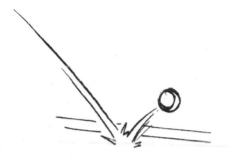

EPIC ATHLETES
SERENA WILLIAMS

EPIC ATHLETES
SERENA WILLIAMS

Dan Wetzel

Illustrations by Sloane Leong

SQUARE
FISH

Henry Holt and Company

New York

**SQUARE
FISH**

An imprint of Macmillan Publishing Group, LLC
120 Broadway, New York, NY 10271
mackids.com

Our books may be purchased in bulk for promotional, educational, or business use. Please
contact your local bookseller or the Macmillan Corporate and Premium Sales Department
at (800) 221-7945 ext. 5442 or by email at MacmillanSpecialMarkets@macmillan.com.

Library of Congress Cataloging-in-Publication Data
Names: Wetzel, Dan, author.
Title: Epic athletes Serena Williams / Dan Wetzel.
Description: New York : Henry Holt and Company, 2019.
| Series: Epic athletes | Audience: Ages 8–12.
Identifiers: LCCN 2018039230 | ISBN 9781250250728 (paperback)
ISBN 9781250295866 (ebook)
Subjects: LCSH: Williams, Serena, 1981– —Juvenile literature.
| Tennis players—United States—Biography—Juvenile literature.
| African American women tennis players—Biography—Juvenile literature.
Classification: LCC GV994.W55 W47 2019 | DDC 796.342092 [B]—dc23
LC record available at https://lccn.loc.gov/2018039230

Originally published in the United States by Henry Holt and Company
First Square Fish edition, 2020
Book designed by Elynn Cohen
Square Fish logo designed by Filomena Tuosto

3 5 7 9 10 8 6 4 2

AR: / LEXILE:

1999 US Open Finals:
Serena Williams vs. Martina Hingis

1

A Superstar Is Born

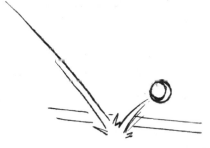

FROM THE FLOOR OF CENTER COURT, Arthur Ashe Stadium rises up in every direction some 120 feet—as tall as an eleven-story building. It includes seating for 23,771 fans in bleachers, grandstands, luxury boxes, and even five restaurants. This is the largest tennis stadium in the world. It may also be the most intimidating.

A row of TV cameras beams the action from the middle of New York City to homes all around the globe. Combine that with all the people seated above in the stands, cheering and shouting down after each point, and it can feel like *everyone* is watching. Some players compare it to playing inside a fishbowl.

The famed asphalt courts are home to some of the most intense competition in tennis. It's where every young player in the world wants to come and win the annual United States Open.

In September 1999, Serena Williams was one of those kids, just seventeen years old at the time.

By almost any equation, Serena wasn't supposed to be there. Not yet, at least. Not ever, perhaps.

Yet there she was, in the women's singles final, serving for match point and a chance to win her first major championship in straight sets over world-class competitor Martina Hingis.

It was a surprise to everyone but Serena and her family. Growing up, her father used to encourage Serena and her older sister Venus to dream. During breaks in practices, he would ask them which of the so-called major tournaments they wanted to win—the US Open, the French Open, the Australian Open, or Wimbledon, which is played outside London, England. Venus always said Wimbledon, the oldest of the events. It is known for its pristine grass courts, white uniforms, and royal family–inspired sophistication.

Serena always shook her head at her sister's answer. "I just said, 'the Open,'" she recalled.

She wanted the wild tournament, the loud tournament, the American tournament. She wanted the toughest one—with fast, hard-surface courts, played in the heat and humidity of August in New York. She wanted to be surrounded by the pressure that comes from all those fans crammed in around you.

Now here she was. She would still be in high school if tennis training hadn't forced her to be homeschooled, allowing her to graduate early. Her fashionable white-and-yellow tennis outfit and her hair pulled back and braided with white beads were signs of her youth. Her ferocious serves and ground game told a story of a kid who, as a player at least, was all grown up.

She was there to prove to herself that she was capable of being a champion. She was there to prove that she was capable of being better than her older sister. Venus, who was one year, three months, and nine days older, had burst onto the scene first and cast such a shadow that Serena was still referred to by many as "Venus's little sister." Serena knew winning the US Open before Venus would go a long way toward changing that. She didn't want to be the little sister. She wanted them together to be known as "the Williams sisters."

To do so, she needed to best Hingis, the number-one-ranked player in the world. Hingis was just nineteen, only a little older than Serena, yet she already owned five major championships. Hingis was classically trained and possessed incredible speed, skill, and shot-making ability. She hailed from Switzerland and was a child prodigy, playing in tournaments by age four. When, at the age of sixteen, Hingis won Wimbledon, she became the youngest singles major champion ever. To defeat her would be an incredible accomplishment.

More than anything, Serena was there to prove that a kid like her could do this.

Serena didn't grow up in a wealthy suburb. She didn't learn the game at a country club. She wasn't part of a youth development program in a tennis-mad community in the United States or Europe, like so many other elite players. The Williamses grew up in Compton, California, an impoverished neighborhood that sits just south of downtown Los Angeles.

They were taught the game by their parents, who learned it by teaching themselves. They were African

Americans in a sport with so few people of color. Their hard-driving father, Richard, got them out on the court at age three because he believed he could create champions who could earn millions.

They never had the best equipment. They were always asking for donations and used to carry milk crates full of old balls out to practice. Eventually, when their supply got too big, they wheeled a beat-up grocery cart onto the court. Even as a toddler, Serena never had a junior-sized racket because it cost too much. She learned to play with an adult racket that was nearly as big as she was. She later credited it with teaching her to swing so hard. There was no other choice. Serena was forced to use every muscle she had to whip it around and smack the ball.

The Williamses practiced not on manicured lawns or glistening private courts but on the cracked concrete of public parks in Compton and the nearby neighborhood of Lynwood.

Serena's father would load the girls into a van, pull up each afternoon to an empty court, and shoo away whoever was hanging around at the time—people dealing drugs, gambling on dice games, or just sleeping on a bench. Then the family would sweep the court clear of broken glass and debris to begin practice. All around, people would stop and stare. This was an unusual sight for Compton: a dad trying to teach his girls tennis. When they practiced, it wasn't uncommon for the sound of gunshots to ring out in the distance. Serena's dad would tell the girls to ignore it or pretend it was just a balloon popping.

At the 1999 US Open, Serena was asked if she ever got distracted. Many of her opponents did when airplanes flew over the courts as they approached nearby LaGuardia Airport. Serena never seemed to blink. It was as though she didn't hear a thing.

"Didn't bother me," she said. "I'm from Compton. I'm used to it. There's just all kinds of other activities going on."

That is how Richard Williams did things. He tried to turn every negative into a positive. As balls wore out and bounced in unexpected directions, for example, he wouldn't replace them because that cost money. Instead, Richard told the girls that it prepared them for when they got older and competed against great players who could put spin on shots. Having old tennis balls was . . . a good thing.

Maybe because of her father's attitude, Serena

never doubted her abilities, at least publicly. She always believed she would play at Arthur Ashe Stadium. Serena always believed she would win the US Open and other major championships.

"When I am on my game, nobody can beat me," Serena said earlier in the tournament. "I think it's impossible for anyone to have a chance against me when I'm playing my best."

Confident comments like that, from a teenager who hadn't yet won a major, bothered some people in tennis. It is a sport that values politeness. The game was first popular with the wealthy and elite of England back in the 1800s. It is a game of honor and sportsmanship, but it also was rooted in a day and age when it was mostly only white people of privilege who played.

Yet here was this seventeen-year-old African American declaring herself unbeatable.

That's the Williamses, though. Richard had long ago stood on one of those Compton courts and announced to a television news crew that his two youngest daughters, then just little kids, would one day dominate women's tennis by winning Grand Slam titles and ranking number one and number two in the world. Prior to this US Open, Richard predicted that Venus and Serena would meet in the finals. A lot of players and fans didn't like such comments.

Hingis heard of the sister-sister championship talk and declared that the entire Williams family had "big mouths." Then, just hours after Serena beat defending champion Lindsay Davenport in her semifinal match, which was the greatest win of Serena's young career, she had to watch Venus, her best friend, suffer a crushing defeat at the hands of Hingis. Serena and Hingis made up before the tournament, but the rivalry was intense.

Venus's loss ended any chance of an all–Williams sisters final. Now Serena was determined not to let Hingis beat them both. Even though the final was scheduled for the next day and Serena had gone through a grueling match against Davenport, she decided to find a practice court and hit some extra balls in preparation. Players usually seek out physical therapy and some rest. Not Serena.

"She's outside practicing?" Hingis said in disbelief. "Go more and get cramps. I'm going to have a massage."

Serena knew she needed to be razor sharp. Hingis was so fast and so accurate with her shots that she would be nearly impossible to beat. Serena entered the US Open as the seventh seed, meaning experts thought six other players were more likely to win. Hingis was the top seed (Venus was third), reaching her third consecutive final. Serena and Hingis had played five times prior to this through the years, with Hingis winning three of the matches.

To win a match in women's tennis, you need to capture two out of three sets. To win a set, you need to win six games. If a set is tied 6–6, then a tiebreaker is held with the first player to seven points (and leading by two points) taking the set. In a match this competitive, every point is important.

Serena came out strong, winning the first set handily, 6–3. Then she took a 5–3 lead in the second set and was on the brink of the title. Her shots were so powerful. Her game was so patient. She needed to win just one of two points to win her first major championship. Hingis was number one for a reason, though. Facing defeat, she rallied and took a point. Then she won another point. Then she took the game, pulling to 5–4. Soon Hingis battled back to 6–6, forcing a tiebreaker.

Suddenly Serena's confidence was rattled. Was she going to blow this? Was she not as good as she thought she was? Could she really do what her big sister couldn't and beat the best player in the world?

Were so many of the doubters right about her and Venus? Can you really be a major champion if you learned the game from your dad on public courts in Compton?

"I was very upset with myself," Serena said. "I was like, 'Serena, this can't happen.'"

If Hingis could claw back and take the second set, she would have all the momentum going into the decisive third set. Serena decided she had to win this title now. She had come too far and worked too hard to fall apart.

"There comes a time when you just have to stop caving," Serena said. "You have to stop. In the end, I told myself, 'You're going to have to perform. Even if you win or lose, you're still going to be out here and you're going to have to perform.'"

She vowed to focus on one shot at a time. She wouldn't think about the chances she had blown. She wouldn't think about the championship that was sitting there waiting to be won. She wouldn't think about all those fans up in the stands, or the television cameras pointed at her, or how the rise of the Williams sisters had electrified women's tennis and caused viewership of the finals to double from the year before.

Serena wouldn't concern herself with her father's predictions or Venus's heartbreak or how she had the historic chance to be the first African American female to win the US Open since Althea Gibson in 1958 and the first African American of any gender since Arthur Ashe (whom the court is named after) in 1975.

Serena would just hit the ball and win the point. And then try it again. And that she did. Tied 4–4 in the tiebreaker, Serena used a powerhouse forehand down the line to take a 5–4 lead. Then, Serena outlasted Hingis in a long rally to get to 6–4. She now had the serve and two chances to win the title. This time she wouldn't let it get away from her.

Serena crushed a serve, estimated to be nearly 120 miles per hour. Hingis was able to return it, but it set Serena up to hammer a backhand that left Hingis on her heels. Hingis was forced to reach just to get it back over the net. Serena then leaned into another backhand, and this one came too hard and too fast for Hingis to deal with. She got a racket on it, but it was hit hard and without any touch. Serena watched it fly too deep and sail over the end line.

Out.

Point for Serena. Game for Serena. Set for

Serena. Match for Serena. Championship for Serena. History for Serena.

The US Open was hers.

Serena clutched her chest, like she was having a heart attack.

"I'm thinking, 'Should I scream? Should I yell? Should I cry?'" she said. "What do you do?"

She wound up doing a little of each. Then she embraced her family, with her parents declaring how excited they were for her. Venus even shared her joy. If Venus wasn't going to win the US Open, at least her younger sister was. (The next day, the two of them would team up to win the doubles championship.) Soon Serena was receiving a phone call from President Bill Clinton, who watched and cheered her on from the White House—"we're all proud of you," Clinton said.

"Really . . . Wow!" Serena said.

Mostly, though, she just kept smiling and clutching that US Open trophy. Here in the proving grounds of New York, with applause thundering down from that giant stadium that rose all around her, the kid from Compton had proved herself indeed.

And she was just getting started.

2

Growing Up in Compton

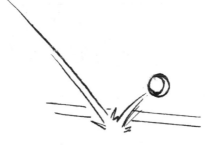

SERENA JAMEKA WILLIAMS was born September 26, 1981, in Saginaw, Michigan. Her parents were Richard and Oracene Williams. Oracene grew up in Michigan, the daughter of an automobile factory worker. She excelled in school and became a registered nurse. Her first husband passed away, and when she met Richard in 1979, she was raising three daughters—Yetunde, Isha, and Lyndrea—on her own.

Richard was raised outside Shreveport,

Louisiana. He was one of six children and grew up in crushing poverty as the son of a sharecropper, which is a very low-paying form of farming that was created in America after the Civil War. In some ways, it was a continuation of the racist policies left over from the era of slavery. There was little opportunity for a poor African American child in the 1940s and 1950s, especially in the Deep South, where racism was rampant. Dr. Martin Luther King Jr. and the civil rights movement wouldn't gain traction until the 1960s.

Blacks and whites lived in separate neighborhoods, drank from separate water fountains, and even ate at separate restaurants. They also had to attend separate schools. The ones for African Americans were almost always underfunded and below the quality of white schools. Making matters even more challenging, Richard's father abandoned the family when Richard was young. With almost no money coming in, Richard, as a boy, had to find ways to help his mother. He set up his own garden and sold fruits and vegetables. He hunted for meat to have at dinner. He did odd jobs around town, pretty much anything that would earn a dollar. He was very determined to build a better life for himself.

As an adult he moved to California, got married, and helped raise six children. After that marriage ended in divorce, Richard was living in Michigan when he met Oracene. They soon married and had two daughters of their own, Venus and Serena. The entire family then decided to move to Southern California, where Richard had lived previously.

There are plenty of places to live in Los Angeles, but Richard chose Compton, a working-class area just ten miles south of downtown. And he did it for a reason.

"I wanted them to grow up tough," Richard told CNN. "There's no place in the world rougher than Compton."

The city of about ninety-five thousand, home to tightly packed streets of houses and businesses, has long been poor and crime-ridden. Especially in the 1980s and 1990s when the Williamses lived there, gangs, violence, and drugs overwhelmed many of its neighborhoods. Just walking to the store, riding a bike to a friend's house, or even sitting on the front steps of your house was a risk.

There were still many working-class families such as Serena's who tried to keep the neighborhood safe and secure, though. Serena's mother took a job as a nurse, and her father opened a small business focused on security. Money was always tight for such a big family, but their small stucco house on Stockton Street, with a chain-link fence surrounding the yard, was a safe spot even as the city remained dangerous.

While many parents try to avoid raising their children in a place such as Compton, or move out when they have the opportunity, it was a choice for Serena's family. Her dad could have moved them to a safer neighborhood, but he wanted his daughters to grow up in such a place so they would realize, as he had as a child in segregated Louisiana, that life can be very challenging.

Richard believed it would open their eyes to the fact that you need to work hard, remain focused, and have a goal. Every day and every decision mattered, Richard would preach. Education was everything. Living a clean, honest life was important. One slip-up could cost you everything. Opportunities were precious and didn't come around all the time.

"He's the type of person that wants to get a job done," Serena said. "He wants to be the best at whatever he does, no matter what it is. He's very determined."

Serena and Venus would, of course, go on to

become professional tennis players. They also pursued college educations when not playing, even delaying their decisions to turn professional to concentrate on high school. And Richard and Oracene were no less proud of their other daughters, who all grew up and became accomplished adults. This is what Richard Williams envisioned when he decided to raise his children in Compton.

The Williamses were a very close family. They tended to do everything together. Tennis would take up a lot of their time, but they were also devoted to their faith. Oracene Williams was a Jehovah's Witness, as were her children. They spent a lot of time learning, reading, and praying. Jehovah's Witnesses follow a form of Christianity, but the religion has some unique elements. Church service is twice a week at what is called "Kingdom Hall." Followers don't observe religious or popular holidays, such as Christmas, Easter, or Halloween, or celebrate individual birthdays. It can be very strict. During free time, the Williamses would often preach and distribute literature about the religion in an effort to attract new followers. Later in life, Serena often pointed to the sky after winning a match and thanked "Jehovah God" for the strength to lead her to victory.

"Being a Jehovah's Witness, we believe in God and the Bible," Serena said. "And without him, I wouldn't be here right now. I really thank him for everything."

There was very little left to chance in Serena's home growing up. With seven people living in one small house, order and discipline were everything. The girls rarely attended parties or played with kids outside of the family. Each sister had a distinct list of chores that needed to be completed. Schoolwork was stressed. Poor grades, even just a single one, could cause tennis or other activities to be taken away. It was the same for not helping with laundry, the dishes, or yardwork.

Serena was the youngest, the baby of the family, which came with its own positives and negatives. She had four older sisters to look after her and adore her. "I was everyone's pet," she wrote years later. She also tried to keep up with her big sisters, who would, like all sisters, tire of her sometimes. She was always closest to Venus, however. Since the family largely kept to themselves, Venus and Serena became best friends.

Their home on Stockton Street contained just two bedrooms, one for the parents and one for all the girls. The kids' room contained two bunk beds.

That's four beds for five kids. Serena not only had to share a room growing up, she even had to share a bed, often with Venus.

The plan for Venus and Serena was set in motion even before they were born. Serena's father had taught himself how to play tennis when he first lived in California. Then, in 1978, while watching the French Open on TV, he heard the announcer say that year's winner, Virginia Ruzici, had just won $40,000 in prize money.

Richard couldn't believe it—he didn't make $40,000 in an entire year! He thought about how hard both he and Serena's mother worked and how little, in comparison, they made. As the family recounts it, the next day Richard told Serena's mother that they needed to have a couple of daughters "and make them into tennis superstars." He vowed to learn more about the game and become their coach. The couples' older three girls were also playing, but Richard believed that he needed to train a kid from a young age to mold her into a champion.

The idea of raising a tennis champion is silly. There is no telling if a baby is going to grow up to be a great athlete or even someone who likes the sport. It was even more far-fetched because of who the Williamses were—namely African Americans from a working-class background, living in a community where tennis was not popular, trying to enter a sport that had a history of discrimination toward people of color.

Tennis had almost exclusively been dominated by white players, both Europeans and Americans. There had been some African American stars through the years, but not many.

There was Arthur Ashe, of course, in the 1960s and 1970s, who was a top player on the pro circuit, winning three Grand Slam titles and serving as an inspiration. Before that, Ora Mae Washington was a dominant player in the 1930s, although she rarely got to play against the great white players of the day.

Althea Gibson was a champion during the 1950s, winning five Grand Slam titles. Even as a brilliant player, life was hard for Althea because of the racism she faced as a black woman. She often had to change for matches in her car because the clubhouses didn't allow African Americans to enter. Other tournaments simply wouldn't let her compete at all. (When Serena was in seventh grade, she wrote a report about Althea, even sending questions to Althea and getting a response.)

For the most part, though, African Americans didn't play tennis, certainly not at the elite level.

While there are tennis courts in nearly every community in the country, to make it as a pro requires hours and hours of training and coaching, which cost money. Most great players come from private tennis clubs and have the resources to learn the game young and train almost every day. For most people, the sport of tennis is not as accessible to play or learn as basketball, football, or soccer.

"For whatever reason, there's this notion that if you didn't grow up around the game, if it wasn't in your blood to begin with, you had no real claim to it," Serena wrote in 2009. "Tennis is like that, I'm afraid. There's a sense of entitlement, of belonging. For the longest time, it was that sense of entitlement that probably kept a whole group of potentially talented minority and underprivileged kids from taking up the game. It must have felt to them like a sport of advantage.

"If your parents didn't play, there was no reason for you to play," Serena continued. "If no one in your community played, you'd never think to reach for a racket in the first place. If you couldn't afford to be a member of some fancy country club, it might never occur to you to teach yourself on some public court."

The Williamses didn't care much for how things

are supposed to go. They had a plan and determination. If tennis had almost exclusively been one way, they were out there in Compton getting ready to turn the entire sport upside down.

East Rancho Dominguez Park sits on the busy corner of Atlantic Avenue and East Compton Boulevard. It is surrounded by a used car lot, a pawn shop, some restaurants, and a tight neighborhood of houses. Traffic buzzes by at all hours of the night. When Serena was growing up, it was known simply as East Compton Park. It sat just over two miles from her family's home. It featured a playground, some weed-strewn fields, a basketball court, a picnic area, and, of course, two tennis courts.

At times, there have been as few as four public tennis courts in the entire city of Compton. That's it. If you want to play tennis in Compton, as the Williamses did back in the 1980s, East Compton Park was pretty much it. Richard jokingly named it the "Compton Hills Country Club" so it sounded like a rich and proper place.

Even with the lack of public courts, almost no one else was there at about three o'clock each afternoon when Richard Williams would drive up in his yellow-and-white Volkswagen minivan, park on the street, and unload his five daughters. Serena's mother would usually join them on her own, after a day of work. The parents would take turns hitting with the girls.

Just because there were few players looking to use the courts doesn't mean no one was there. While the Williamses saw the spot on a busy corner as a place to play tennis, gangs saw it as a place to deal drugs just outside the view of police. In his autobiography, Richard Williams tells the story of having to fight gang members so that he could use the court, even suffering broken ribs and losing teeth. Eventually, he said he even brought a gun to the court to scare them away.

As time went on, it became clear that this determined dad was going to return, day after day, with his daughters. Eventually the gangs got the message and moved to another Compton corner. These were, unofficially, the Williams family courts. Everyone in the area began to respect this father and mother trying to teach their kids the game of tennis.

"It had taken nearly two years and almost destroyed my body," Richard wrote in the book *Black and White: The Way I See It.* "But in that moment, none of that mattered. What mattered was the courts were ours."

The Williams sisters became a local curiosity. They were a group playing an unusual game for the neighborhood. Yet even nonfans could watch them hitting the ball hard and realize there was something special going on. That became particularly true as Venus and Serena, by far the most talented of the children, grew up. The same gangs and drug dealers who once harassed the family and tried to scare them away began to protect and look out for them. That's how Compton could be. While living in the city was rough and could tear people down, Compton also took pride in the ones who went on to have success.

Serena was literally raised on a tennis court. As a toddler, before she was strong enough to swing a racket, she watched or chased balls. Richard patterned his coaching system on what he saw in training videos. He'd put the girls through the same drills and training sessions, heavy on repetition, all under his watchful eye. Serena's dad was strict, and he didn't tolerate lapses of concentration or poor effort. If you were there to work, you would work hard.

When Serena was three years old, her father

decided she was ready to do more than just fetch balls. It was time to take a swing. Little Serena was handed a racket that was nearly as big as she was because her family considered it a waste of money to buy a youth racket she'd quickly outgrow. She found a way to muscle it around and hit the ball. With that, she began training, at least for a few minutes, almost every day. Her mom or dad would lob balls and Serena would take a mighty swing. She often missed the ball or whacked it into the net, but even at a very young age, there were signs that she was uniquely coordinated.

As the years went on and Venus and Serena grew older and stronger, it was common for them to hit hundreds of balls in a day, sometimes even five hundred. Richard had studied up on the perfect form for hitting a tennis ball and tried to teach the girls through repetition. As they hit and hit and hit, he would watch closely and bark out comments at the slightest imperfection. Soon it became routine to not just smack the ball back over the net, but to place it on the area of the court precisely where they wanted it to land. The first goal was to force their opponent to move, something young players struggle to master. As they slowly added power to each attempt, accurate returns then became winners—

balls that an opponent was unable to reach and return.

Another focus was the serve. Serena was required to work on hers at the end of every practice, when she was already tired, because without a reliable serve, especially in tough moments during a match, nothing else really matters. It is the only shot in tennis that the player completely controls. Special attention was paid to how Serena tossed the ball in the air. Oftentimes the way a player tosses the ball will reveal where they are going to hit the ball, either just inside the center service line, or outside just inside the sideline. By learning to throw it up the exact same way every time, it allowed Serena to disguise where she was going to place the shot.

While tennis was an obsession for the family, it wasn't Serena's only sport. She also took gymnastics lessons. She was constantly tumbling and pulling off cartwheels and round-offs, often inside the family's cramped living room. While that drove her parents crazy, the flexibility and strength that gymnastics generated aided her tennis game as well. Serena also enjoyed swimming, running track, and riding her bike with Venus.

Like for most kids, life was busy. It was about to get even busier.

3

Best Friends and Competitors

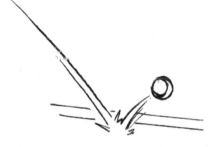

WHEN VENUS WAS NINE, Richard decided she was ready to play in competitive tournaments run by the United States Tennis Association (USTA). He still thought Serena was too young. Previously the sisters had only participated in small local events. They were basically just for fun and were designed to offer participants an opportunity to gain some game experience. Richard believed those were enough for little kids, because he thought that developing fundamentals was more important than dealing with the pressure and expectations of actual tournaments. Practice makes perfect, after all.

Most serious players begin participating in competitive events by the time they are six or seven. By the age of nine, a pecking order of the best local players is usually established, and the very best of that group quickly move on to the national scene in search of top competition. The USTA also sponsors a "youth progression" series of events across the country for players as young as seven. Its national junior circuit of tournaments begins with players twelve years old and younger.

While there had been some buzz about two sisters from Compton with great potential, very few people had seen them play because they had avoided the bigger tournaments and didn't train with a well-known coach or at a prestigious tennis program or club. They were a mystery.

That would change as Venus entered her first tournament. It was obvious those long afternoons of practice had worked. Venus was tall for her age, and the power with which she hit the ball was too much for her opponents to handle. Her fundamentals were also pretty good. She was confident in her game. Even though this was Venus's first-ever tournament, she won. Then she entered in another and won that one, also. Southern California has one of the strongest local tennis communities in the country, but the other kids were no match for Venus. Even as she began playing opponents a year or two older, Venus kept winning.

Serena was excited for her older sister. She loved watching her play and win. She wanted to play, too, though. Just standing outside the court cheering wasn't enough. Seeing Venus do well made Serena think she, too, could do well.

Her father wouldn't allow it. He believed that young players focus too much on winning junior tournaments and not enough on training. The goal wasn't to win a USTA junior event. It was to win the US Open or Wimbledon.

But Serena was impatient. One day she noticed a tournament sign-up sheet arrive in the mail for Venus. For some reason, there were actually two of them. Desperate to play, Serena took the extra one and filled out her name, found an envelope and a stamp, and mailed it in without telling her parents. While she didn't include the tournament registration fee, she figured she would just see what happened.

When the tournament was set to begin, Serena tagged along in full outfit and carrying her racket.

No one in her family thought anything of it. Then the tournament director announced a match and said "Serena Williams" should report to a certain court. Richard couldn't believe his ears and thought the director had made a mistake, but he was informed that both Venus and Serena Williams were registered.

Richard tried to ask his daughter what she had done, but she just ran off to play. At that point, there was nothing her father could do. He wasn't going to stop the tournament and admit his daughter had signed up behind his back. In the end, Richard was excited that she was so driven and competitive, even if it meant he had to find an additional forty dollars in entry fees. He went and watched the match, only to see Serena win.

"Look at you," Richard said, according to Serena. He was proud. Serena was excited. She was the youngest player there, just an eight-year-old playing against kids as old as ten. She was competing in a tournament for the first time. Her mom and dad offered pointers for the next match. She won that, too. Then she won the next match to reach the final. That's when the winning ended, but only because of who her opponent was—Venus. It was the first time the two sisters met in the finals of a tournament. It would be far from the last. Venus was too good for Serena at this point, winning 6–2, 6–2.

Afterward, they gave Venus a gold trophy for being the champion and Serena a silver trophy for being the runner-up. Serena kept looking at the gold champion's trophy. She wanted it, not the silver. Venus, ever the kind and supportive big sister, offered to trade. Seeing Serena happy was more important to Venus than the color of the trophy. Serena took the deal.

That was their relationship in a nutshell. Despite being only slightly older, Venus was protective. She cared about Serena's feelings. She wanted to encourage Serena in every way possible. She was always looking out for Serena.

One day, Serena went to school without her lunch money. The rule was if you didn't have any money, you could get a peanut butter and jelly sandwich, but not the main, hot meal. That day, the cafeteria was serving Serena and Venus's favorite, fried chicken. Serena said she was so upset about getting stuck with peanut butter and jelly that she went and told Venus about not having any money. Without hesitation, Venus gave Serena her lunch money and volunteered to have the sandwich instead. Anything for her little sister.

"She said, 'you go eat,'" Serena recalled years later on *The Oprah Winfrey Show*.

In return, Serena idolized Venus. She would follow Venus around and try to mimic everything she did. If Venus had a favorite color, Serena would make it her favorite color, also. If Venus had a favorite animal, it was soon Serena's favorite, too. They became so attached their parents started to worry. Serena needed to have her own interests and opinions. She couldn't just copycat Venus. When the family went out to eat at a restaurant, Serena would only eat whatever Venus was eating. A solution was hatched.

"My parents would make me order first," Serena told Oprah. "But then when [Venus would] order, I'd just change my order."

The love the sisters shared was one reason that they didn't like to practice against each other, let alone play each other in tournaments. If they met up, then that meant one of them was going to lose. At this age, it meant Serena. As a kid, fifteen months is a significant age difference. Plus, Venus was bigger and stronger than opponents a year or two older than she was, let alone her own age or younger.

Serena was shorter, and though powerful for her age, she was not as talented as her big sister.

"It was really difficult to play her at first because she would always beat me," Serena said. "I had to go out there and improve."

Their parents didn't like them playing, either. First, they wanted Serena to grow confident as a player and not get crushed every time by Venus. Second, there was the fear that if Serena did improve enough to beat Venus, it might rattle Venus's confidence. Or Venus, being sensitive to her sister's feelings, would go easy on her and not get the most out of playing. Finally, there's an old saying for parents—you're only as happy as your least-happy child. When one wins and the other loses, parents will feel bad for the disappointed child and won't be able to celebrate with the victorious one.

"You're always supporting the one that is down in that moment because you don't want to see either of them lose," their mother said on *Oprah*.

The solution was to avoid lots of direct practicing against each other. Instead they took turns hitting with their father. They also moved Venus, despite being just nine years old, into the under-12 division. Serena, at age eight, would play in the under-10 division. That way, at least for now, they wouldn't play each other. For Venus, the older competition was a little tougher, but it didn't really matter. She never lost anyway. Venus would win all the sixty-three junior tournaments that she entered from the ages of nine to eleven. Serena was nearly as good, finishing 46–3, with one of those defeats coming against Venus.

In most cases, when players are dominating local tournaments the way Venus and Serena were, their parents and coaches move them up to the national circuit to find the strongest and most experienced competition. Richard, as both parent and coach, didn't believe in that, however. It would mean a lot of travel and a lot of money. It would mean time away from school and practice. Maybe the local tournaments were too easy, but he wasn't going to budge.

As the Williams sisters racked up tournament title after tournament title in Southern California, they no longer operated in anonymity. Venus was considered a prodigy and a future star in the sport. Even though the sisters weren't playing nationally, stories began appearing in newspapers and on TV about the family and their unusual story—two talented daughters taught by their parents in an area not known for tennis.

The publicity generated a lot of curiosity. More and more people came to watch the Williams sisters in local tournaments. They always left impressed. Suddenly opportunities to meet tennis celebrities and hit balls with star players began presenting themselves. Serena and Venus jumped at the chance to meet Billie Jean King, Jimmy Connors, Chris Evert, Zina Garrison, and others.

They also no longer struggled to find suitable equipment. Their home overflowed with rackets, ball machines, shoes, outfits, and other accessories that manufacturers shipped free to the family. Venus was just ten, Serena nine. Even though they were years away from turning professional, companies hoped giving them free equipment now might entice them to one day sign an endorsement contract. They no longer needed that old shopping cart full of worn-down balls, although Richard liked to keep it around anyway.

As the two ripped through the competition in Los Angeles and turned up in the media, the future of tennis was clear. Maybe they weren't out on the national circuit, maybe they did things differently than others, maybe there was still a lot to learn, but the Williams sisters were coming.

4

Opportunity

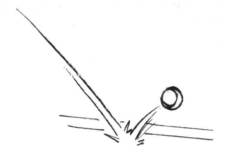

BY 1991, AS VENUS AND SERENA were dominating local tennis tournaments, Richard realized that he needed help coaching them. Richard had proven to be a good coach, but he lacked experience developing a professional player, let alone a Grand Slam champion. While neither Venus nor Serena had played on the national junior circuit, anyone who saw them at events in Southern California knew they had serious potential. Word began to spread, even all the way to the East Coast.

Rick Macci ran a tennis academy in Haines City, Florida, not far from Orlando. He was in his mid-thirties and had a reputation as not just one of the best coaches in America, but one who was particularly good at training young players with incredible natural talent.

His most famous student was Jennifer Capriati, a New York native who began working with Rick in 1987. She was just ten years old at the time. Jennifer had a powerful game but lacked flexibility and precision in her shot-making and possessed just an average serve. Rick began hours of daily training built on changing that. Some of it was simply hitting hundreds of balls or studying great champions. Other ideas were unusual, even seemingly silly. Rick would have Jennifer throw a football to simulate the motion of tossing a tennis ball in the air before a serve. Another drill designed to increase racket speed called for Jennifer to stand just a few feet from the fence surrounding the court, place each foot in a ball hopper (a basket used to collect tennis balls), and try to hit balls down onto the court with enough power to bounce them up and over the fence.

The methods worked and Jennifer's game soared. After just a few years training with Rick, she became advanced enough to turn pro at the age of thirteen.

Jennifer would eventually go on to win three Grand Slam singles titles, reach number one in the world rankings, and make millions of dollars.

Rick's track record with Jennifer convinced Richard Williams, in 1991, to call Rick and ask if he was interested in coaching Venus and Serena. Since lots of parents wanted Rick to train their son or daughter, his challenge was figuring out who was a legitimate prospect and who was overrated. Rick could only teach so many players, so he limited his academy to around thirty players and never more than forty. He took great pride in spending hours and hours with them.

When a request would come in, Rick would check the player's national ranking and get a sense of their basic ability. Or he might go to a major event on the national junior circuit and watch them play. The Williams sisters didn't compete on that level, though. They were still local. They had no national ranking. Normally, Rick wouldn't have considered such players, but he, just like every other coach in the country, had heard a little about Venus. Serena was, at the time, just Venus's younger sister. Serena had to accept that all the attention was on her older sister.

"It never really bothered me at all," Serena said. "I've always been in the background. I always like the background . . . Venus, she's always been in the front. She's always going to be Venus. I'm always going to be Serena."

One person who did believe in Serena was her father. He repeatedly told reporters and television crews that he thought Serena would be better than Venus, even if no one else saw it at the time. His reasoning was that Venus was winning due to her superior strength, but Serena was learning how to hit the shots that would be more valuable in the professional ranks, where everyone is strong.

"Serena couldn't beat [opponents] with power," Richard said. "She had to learn to do angles and drop shots."

While Richard would talk up Serena in the media, he would never say it directly to the girls. He never played favorites. They weren't certain he even meant what he was telling reporters.

"He never told me I would be better than Venus," Serena said. "He said that so people [would] start paying attention to me, not just see me as Venus's younger sister. It's not like any dad to go up to one daughter and say, 'You're going to be better than this person over here.'"

Richard's promoting must've paid off, because Rick accepted his invitation to make the cross-country trip to Los Angeles to scout the girls in person. If nothing else, he was curious.

Rick arrived at night and met with Richard, Oracene, and the girls. They talked tennis. They talked teaching. They talked about how Richard still wanted to be the girls' primary coach, but how Rick could work alongside him. Meanwhile, Rick talked about Jennifer Capriati and showed pictures of his tennis academy, complete with gleaming courts, baskets of fresh balls, and trees all around. Venus and Serena practically drooled at what they were seeing. This would be quite different than the "Compton Hills Country Club."

Venus and Serena were young, but they recognized this was a big moment in their lives. Rick was an important person who had traveled a long way to see them. They knew who Jennifer Capriati was, and they understood that they needed a coach like Rick to get them to that level. This was their chance to make it happen.

They would need to play their best. Serena and Venus were confident players, but this was no longer about beating some kid in a local tournament. This was about getting Rick to choose them over all the other top young players in the country. Were they really as good as they believed? Or were they just good on the local level? Could a champion really come out of Compton, a champion trained by their self-taught father and not at some big, fancy club?

Richard said he would pick Rick up the next day in the Volkswagen van and take him to the "Compton Hills Country Club." Rick later wrote in his autobiography that he thought it would be an actual country club. When the van pulled up alongside East Compton Boulevard, Rick was stunned at what he saw.

"There were about twenty guys playing basketball, and there were another fifteen people at least passed out on the grass," Rick recalled in his book. "There was broken glass and beer bottles everywhere. This was definitely different than the luxurious Grenelefe Golf and Tennis Resort where I was director of tennis. So it was really a culture shock to see the situation."

Suddenly, Rick wasn't sure if the trip was worth it. This was like nothing he had ever experienced. His uneasiness grew as he started feeding balls to Venus and Serena. Both girls struck the ball well, but their fundamentals weren't at the level Rick was used to seeing. They were good players. Richard had done a decent job. They had been taught the game fairly well. There was no question that they had potential.

However, they clearly had not been trained by top-line coaches at high-priced academies. Their swings were slightly sloppy and a little inconsistent. Their footwork wasn't right. They were relying on athletic ability rather than proper training. Rick began regretting his decision to visit the Williamses. He began to wonder if the reason Richard hadn't put them on the national circuit was that he was trying to hide them from elite competition.

"I'm looking at this and I'm thinking, 'This is a train wreck!'" Rick wrote. "'This is all hype and I cannot believe I'm in Compton, California, ruining my weekend.' I didn't think they were really that good . . . I thought Venus and Serena looked like decent athletes but technically they were all over the map, just because they were improvising. You could tell they just didn't have quality instruction."

Venus and Serena kept hitting the balls, doing their best to impress Rick. They didn't know that he now had doubts about their future. Nor did they realize that if Rick turned them down, so, too, might other coaches who would hear about Rick's decision, be scared off, and never bother coming to Compton to scout them.

Rick wasn't going to just leave right away, though. People he respected had raved about seeing Venus and Serena in tournaments. He decided that rather than continue with hitting drills, he would try to watch them play in an actual game. Maybe there was something he was missing. As much as Rick wanted to see their ability, he also wanted to try to measure their heart. There is no better way to do that than through competition.

In an instant, everything changed. The girls may not have perfected their form, but they chased down every shot, fought for points, and looked like completely different players when they were trying to win rather than just train. Venus and Serena were competitors. They hated to lose. It was like night and day.

"Their stock rose immediately," Rick wrote. "You don't judge a book by its cover. I looked cosmetically and I saw what I wanted to see . . . I thought they were limited. Now when they started competing, I saw the preparation get a little quicker, I saw the footwork get a little faster, I saw consistency raise a little higher . . . to me their stock rose even more. To me that's always the X factor, the way someone competes. Venus and Serena had a deep-down burning desire to fight and compete at this age. It was unique. Unreal hunger."

Rick no longer regretted making the trip to

Compton. The Williams sisters were strong, fast, and determined. Rick Macci knew he could teach the rest and iron out the imperfections. He loved that they wanted so desperately to learn how to be great. He wanted the family to move to Florida and come to his tennis academy.

At one point during their game, the girls decided to take a break. Rick and Richard were talking when Venus came over and asked for permission to use the bathroom. Richard said yes. Rather than jog off the court, Venus instead turned a couple of cart-wheels and even walked on her hands, showing unusual athletic ability and coordination. Rick was in awe. His mind began dreaming beyond tennis to the biggest sports star in the world at the time, Michael Jordan of the NBA Chicago Bulls.

"I said [to Richard], 'Let me tell you something,'" Rick wrote later. "'I think you have the next female Michael Jordan on your hands.'"

Richard, forever protective and promoting Serena, too, reminded Rick that he would eventually realize just how lucky he was to get to work with Venus *and* Serena.

"No," Richard said, "I've got the next *two* Michael Jordans."

5

Florida

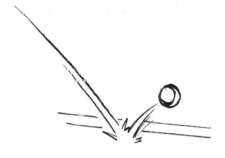

THE GRENELEFE GOLF and Tennis Resort sits next to Lake Marion in the central part of Florida, about halfway between Orlando and Tampa. In the early 1990s, it featured three plush golf courses with more than four hundred condominiums lining the fairways. There was a massive clubhouse and banquet center, four separate swimming pools, and, of course, twenty-two gleaming tennis courts shaded by a cypress tree grove.

The Williams sisters were not in Compton anymore.

The area was quiet. There were a lot of orange trees and retirees. Gone was the noise, traffic, and danger of their old neighborhood. There would be no more sweeping the courts or shooing away drug dealers. There was never gunfire ringing out in the distance. The Williamses had uprooted their life from Los Angeles in search of the perfect tennis environment. This was it.

The courts were new. The balls were new. All the equipment and gear and training techniques were new. There was now no need to concentrate on anything but improving their games. The girls would go to school until about one p.m. and then start training five to six hours a day under the blistering Florida sun. It was fun. It was exciting. That isn't to say the move was easy. Serena had to leave her school, her friends, the family's faith community, and the familiarity of Compton. Maybe back home wasn't the ideal place to learn the game, but it was where *she* had learned the game. It was all she knew.

Then there was Rick Macci, who ran about with endless energy, darting from one court to the next, working with this student and that. He blared music over outdoor speakers to keep the excitement up. He wanted everything to be fast-paced and focused. He believed in doing everything perfectly, and his work ethic matched that of Venus and Serena, who were excited to get the most out of their time in Florida. When one wasn't working with Rick, they still worked with their dad. There were other coaches, too, personal hitting instructors who wouldn't tolerate even the slightest error in their swings.

In Florida, the coaches noticed everything—footwork, balance, grip, form, you name it. Training like that can be frustrating, but it is the only way to achieve greatness. The difference between making it as a pro and falling a bit short can be just a couple of points a match. The same goes with advancing to, let alone winning, a Grand Slam. There is no room for error.

The sisters' mother and father were worried about one thing—that tennis might be too big a part of their life. They didn't want their daughters burning out or feeling undue pressure to perform. The family was pursuing tennis careers in a very serious manner—if not, why move to Florida? Still, it couldn't be the only thing in their lives.

Before she became a nurse, Serena's mother used

to be a teacher, and Serena's father was always saying that the only true way out of poverty is through an education. Richard had grown up attending segregated schools that were of very poor quality. He thought it was shameful to not embrace the academic opportunities now afforded African Americans. Serena and Venus took the toughest classes possible, including extra languages, eventually becoming fluent in not just English, but also French and Italian. They were expected to earn straight As, and their parents would take tennis away from them if they slipped at all. When Serena talked of being a veterinarian, they encouraged her. When she wanted to enroll in a gymnastics, ballet, or karate class, they signed her up.

This was one of the reasons Richard decided to keep both Venus and Serena out of all junior competition. "Running to a junior tournament every weekend, forgetting the rest of your family is not the way," Richard said. "Forgetting about education is the wrong way."

He didn't like the pressure to win that parents and coaches put on young players. Richard also thought that the constant traveling to events was a waste of time and money—why not stay home and work on fundamentals or hit with the coaches and older boys at the academy who were better players than the girls on the circuit? He didn't think winning a junior tournament even mattered much. All a trophy did, according to Richard, was cause someone to look backward on past accomplishment, not forward to future ones.

"I do not allow any trophies in my house," Richard said back in 1999. "I've never allowed one trophy in the house at any time. I put all the trophies in the garage."

There was more to it, also. Richard and Oracene didn't like to have the girls play against each other because it would lift one up while making the other feel bad. While this would be unavoidable at the professional level, being able to avoid this as young kids would be beneficial.

"I learned that it wouldn't be good to enter Venus in this tournament and Serena in this tournament because we wanted two girls to grow up with a bunch of love for each other," Richard said. "And that love needed to be cultivated and developed, and it needed time to do so."

While all this made sense to the Williams family, it didn't to the outside tennis world. Richard bore the brunt of the criticism from other parents and coaches. If he was going to say they were wrong for sending their kids to junior tournaments or question their value system and the way they taught their daughters, then they were going to criticize him back.

Some thought Richard was stunting the growth of Venus and Serena by keeping them from competitive tournaments. Others claimed it was actually Richard who was taking tennis too seriously since most kids find the junior circuit a fun break from hours and hours of dull training. Still, others questioned why Richard and Rick Macci would have the girls practice with boys who could overwhelm them.

At the time, having girls practice almost exclusively with boys was rare. Serena thought it was a good idea, though. Yes, the boys, especially the fourteen- and fifteen-year-olds at the academy, could overpower her. When they played matches, she'd always lose, usually 6–0, 6–0. Winning wasn't the point, though. Serena had to learn to adapt and, at the same time, raise her power to compete with them. Winning points and occasionally games was a sign of progress.

"If there's faster, harder, stronger competition

out there to help you fire up your game, you should absolutely take advantage of it," Serena wrote. "Boys, girls, it shouldn't matter."

After a couple of years at Grenelefe with Rick Macci, the Williamses decided to move again, this time to Pompano Beach, Florida, which is near Miami in the southern part of the state. Richard would again be the girls' primary coach, although they would still work with hitting instructors and other top teachers. That included staying in touch with Rick, but also linking up with Nick Bollettieri, who was a famous coach out of Bradenton, Florida. Nick had worked with numerous champions, including Monica Seles and Andre Agassi. Venus and Serena would travel to learn from Nick, or he would come and pay them a visit.

By taking over again as their main coach, Richard invited even more second-guessing from other tennis players, parents, officials, fans, and the media. How could a father get the most out of these girls? Would this cost Venus and Serena their careers? By not playing on the junior circuit, is he hiding them because they aren't that good? Everyone else seemed to know what was best for the Williamses. But Serena trusted her father and knew how quickly her game was developing. He was confident, so she was confident.

"I've always thought this was a genius move," Serena wrote years later of not playing on the junior circuit. "It's one of the reasons Venus and I are still going strong. It kept us from burning out on tennis at an early age and it allowed us to develop our games in an exciting new way."

The family still felt the negative attention. They were different. Tennis was a mostly white, suburban sport. They were African Americans from the inner city. They went about things in their own way. Richard was outspoken and unapologetic. And not everyone in the tennis world liked that. As with everything, the Williamses leaned on one another and kept working.

"My dad always said negative attention is better than no attention," Serena said. "As long as the truth lives inside of us and we know what the truth is, that stuff really doesn't bother you. It doesn't really matter."

Results are what matter. And soon enough, Venus and Serena would deliver those.

30-40

Championship Point #2

The match continues...

6

Turning Pro

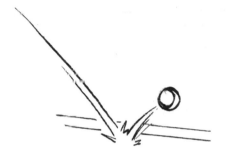

IN THE 1990S, tennis players could turn pro at thirteen. (Can you imagine playing against Serena Williams at that age?!) As young as that sounds, there were teenagers who were capable of competing on the Women's Tennis Association (WTA) Tour. Jennifer Capriati, one of Rick Macci's pupils, was one of them, becoming an instant contender. However, by age seventeen, Capriati was struggling with the pressure of being a pro. She suffered from burnout, depression, and other off-court issues. She had run-ins with the police. Over a two-year period in 1993 and 1994, she stepped away from tennis completely, playing just one event. While she later returned to the game and reached number one in the rankings, at the time she was considered a cautionary tale of the pitfalls of kids going pro when they're too young.

Even without Jennifer serving as a warning, Venus and Serena's parents were not in favor of their daughters becoming pro players until they were at least sixteen and finished with high school (with homeschooling, the girls would be done early). Perhaps they'd even start college before joining the tour.

Tennis could wait.

The WTA agreed with that thinking and in 1994, partially to guard against another Jennifer Capriati, decided to change its rules. It would slowly increase the minimum age to turn pro until it eventually rose to eighteen (the WTA has since altered its age eligibility rules). As a result, Venus, who was about to turn fourteen, was forced into a decision. She either needed to turn pro before the new age limit was enacted, or risk having to wait until she was eighteen to play full-time on the WTA Tour.

Waiting that long was too much. By playing just

one pro tournament now, Venus could control how much she played over the next few years. Without much choice, Venus entered a WTA Tournament in Oakland called the Bank of the West Classic. It was 1994, and the plan called for her to play this one event, beat the deadline for becoming a pro, and then return to her "normal" life in Florida. She would maybe play in a couple of WTA events a year.

The anticipation from the media and fans was enormous. Venus was a well-known name in tennis but hadn't played in an actual tournament since she was eleven years old back in California. Since all eyes were going to be on Venus, Rick Macci, who still worked with the girls, called Richard Williams up and said it was time to ramp up the training and get Venus ready. Instead, Richard, concerned about the mounting pressure, took the girls to Disney World for a week to relax.

The benefit of officially becoming a professional, however, was that if Venus proved herself, money would no longer be an issue because she could sign lucrative endorsement deals with big-name sports apparel companies. Richard could have agreed to deals the moment Venus turned pro, but instead he gambled that she would do well enough in her first event that she would earn even more money from companies desperate to be associated with her. For the Bank of the West Classic, Venus wore a tennis outfit purchased at J. C. Penney and used a racket with no logo on it.

Venus's pro debut was huge news. The tournament rarely received much media attention. This time there were reporters from ESPN, CNN, and major newspapers around the world. It was all because of Venus. Matched up against Shaun Stafford, a former college tennis champion ranked fifty-seventh in the world at the time, Venus played great, winning the match in two sets, 6–3, 6–4. She jumped up and down in excitement at the end. "It was impressive," Stafford said.

"I wasn't nervous," Venus said after. "I know I can play."

Next up was Arantxa Sánchez Vicario, who had won the US and French Opens and was ranked number one in the world at the time. Surely, everyone thought, Venus was going to get run off the court by the best player on earth.

Instead Venus won the first set, 6–3. Then she took a 3–1 lead in the second set. The fans and media couldn't believe it. Could a fourteen-year-old who had nontraditional training and hadn't played on the junior circuit beat the world number one?

Sánchez Vicario, twenty-two, was a Grand Slam champion for a reason, though. She won the next game, and then she broke Venus's serve to make it 3–3. From there, she turned it on. Venus got rattled and didn't win another game. Sánchez Vicario wound up forcing a third set and winning 3–6, 6–3, 6–0.

That was okay. While Venus lost, the tennis world was impressed. The hype was real. No one doubted the Williams sisters anymore.

Within months, Nike offered Venus a $12 million endorsement deal to wear its clothing. It was banking on Venus being a superstar and would gladly pay her even if it had to wait until she was ready to play a full-time professional schedule. It was just one of many deals that were made. Richard's gamble paid off. Even with the early success, Venus went back to finishing her schooling and training in Florida. She didn't enter another tournament in 1994 and competed in just three in 1995 and five in 1996.

For Serena, watching the excitement surrounding her sister made her eager to become a professional, also. There was little to no jealousy or bitterness about Venus getting the attention. "We're best friends," Serena said. Still, there was anticipation. When would it be her turn? When would she get her chance? When would she be allowed to compete and show not just the world, but herself, what she was capable of doing? At that point, all eyes were on Venus. No one was talking about Serena.

"[Venus] was 'the Next Big Thing,'" Serena wrote. "I was still just 'the Next Big Thing's Kid Sister.'"

Serena knew that even when she did turn pro, she was going to follow the slow and steady plan, also. Her big day came in October 1995, when Richard entered her in the Bell Challenge in Quebec City, Canada. Just like when Venus competed at the Bank of the West Classic, the goal of the event for Serena was simply to turn pro before the WTA age eligibility deadline so she wouldn't have to wait until she was eighteen to become a full-time professional. That she accomplished. Almost nothing else went well.

The tournament wasn't nearly the big deal it was when Venus became a pro. First off, it was a qualifying match that was held at a local indoor tennis club, not an actual stadium with fans, announcers, or much media. Serena would have to win the qualifying match just to get to the regular tournament, which wasn't even a well-known competition. Worse yet, Serena and Richard had trouble flying to Canada and arrived late the night before, so there was no time to practice.

Serena played Annie Miller, an eighteen-year-old, and lost quickly, 6–1, 6–1. The entire match took less than an hour. It was an underwhelming start to her career. Serena jokes now that she is glad no one filmed the match because it would live on YouTube forever. Serena hadn't played in a single tournament in more than four years, and she looked inexperienced.

"I felt bad out there because I lost," Serena said that night. "I played kind of like an amateur."

Miller agreed. "She needs to play some junior events. There's no substitute for the real thing."

Serena was disappointed but undeterred. She would not change her plan, though, and start competing in junior events like Annie Miller suggested. She would go back to high school and practice her fundamentals. If there was one thing that losing to Annie taught her, it was that her father was correct. Serena wasn't ready to be a full-time professional tennis player. She wouldn't even enter another tournament in 1995 or 1996. Her family wanted her to relax and train and enjoy being a kid.

"I'm just afraid, especially with Serena, who's a perfectionist, that she'll take it so seriously that she'll never have fun with it, be a flop at eighteen," Richard told the *New York Times*.

No matter how many people were demanding more and more out of the Williamses, Richard and Oracene weren't going to change the plan now. Success could wait. Too soon might be too much. Education was still the most important thing. They kept getting criticized for everything they did, but they were determined to tune out the critics and do what was best for their daughters.

"I only allowed Venus and Serena to play very sparingly," Richard said. "When Venus wanted to play, I wouldn't let her play. When she was fourteen, she said, 'I can play six tournaments.' I [said], 'You can play one tournament. You're going to get an education.'"

Patience. The winning would come.

7

Upswing

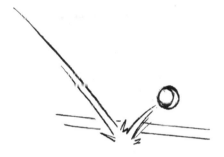

FROM 1995 TO ABOUT 1998, Venus and Serena focused on their education while slowly becoming bigger presences on the WTA Tour. After a few years of homeschooling, they switched to the more traditional Driftwood Academy in Lake Park, Florida. After graduation, they both began attending college and studying fashion design at the Art Institute of Fort Lauderdale. As Venus approached eighteen and Serena seventeen, they soon built a house near their parents' and moved in together. (Venus would do most of the cooking.)

Their mother would have preferred waiting until they were even older, but it was clear they were growing up and ready to become true professional tennis players. As a singles player in the 1997 US Open, Venus, at the age of seventeen, reached the finals before losing to Martina Hingis. Serena, meanwhile, began asserting herself, reaching the semifinals of a WTA event in Chicago by defeating top-ten-ranked players Monica Seles and Mary Pierce. As a doubles team, they quickly became a factor, winning games and even tour event championships in 1998.

In 1999, Serena, who was seventeen at the time, entered the Open Gaz de France, which was held in Paris. It was considered a Tier II WTA event, which means not a major tournament (Tier I) or a Grand Slam (Australian Open, French Open, US Open, and Wimbledon). Venus was playing that same week in a bigger tournament (a Tier I event) in Oklahoma City, Oklahoma. As always, Richard didn't like entering them in the same competition unless it was absolutely necessary.

Though the Open Gaz was not the most prestigious event, it did feature number-one-ranked Hingis (she was upset in the quarterfinals). Serena was not successful enough to be ranked nationally yet and thus not considered much of a contender. Serena began playing some of her best tennis, however, rolling to the finals—without dropping a single set! It was an impressive display, especially for someone so young. Suddenly everyone was talking about the younger Williams sister.

In the finals, she matched up against Amélie Mauresmo, a great player and future two-time Grand Slam winner. Serena won the first set 6–2. Then Amélie stormed back and won the second 6–3. The third set was tied at 6–6 before going to a tiebreaker. Whoever could score seven points first (and win by two or more) would take the championship.

Having come this far, Serena pushed herself to dig deep. This was the most pressure she'd faced in a tournament, so she thought back to all her training, all her practice, all the times she pushed herself through extra drills or serves by dreaming that it was for a tournament championship. Here she was now, no longer dreaming, but living the reality.

It worked. Serena won the tiebreaker 7–4 to capture her first professional singles title! That same day, Venus won the tournament in Oklahoma City, making the Williamses the first sisters ever to each win a professional tournament in the same week.

Soon after, Serena defeated the great Steffi Graf to win her first Tier I WTA event, the Evert Cup, played in Indian Wells, California, near Palm Springs. Her career was starting to take off.

"This win means a lot to me because Steffi is a great champion," Serena told reporters. "This is the biggest tournament I've ever won. I know that I can win the big ones now."

This was Serena's breakout year. She would enter twelve tournaments and win five—including that historic US Open championship mentioned in the first chapter. By the end of the year, Venus was ranked third and Serena fourth (Martina Hingis was still number one).

Venus's and Serena's stars were soaring, and their fan bases began to explode. They had considerable support, especially from African American fans who were drawn to the game because there was someone who looked like them playing it. Many fans of all races loved their underdog story, the family ties, and the historic nature of their rise. There were still plenty who rooted against them or were uncomfortable with Richard's strong comments and unapologetic approach, but there were also adoring crowds wherever they went. Serena signed an endorsement deal with Puma, which outfitted her in modern styles that shook the sport up. Younger fans loved it. So, too, did Serena, who was passionate about fashion and would offer input on designs and color schemes.

There was also a playful side to the sisters. While they were becoming formidable challengers on the court, they were still young and inquisitive about how the world around them worked. Still a bit overwhelmed and too shy to always ask for advice from other, more experienced players, Venus came up with the idea of starting their own newsletter, *Tennis Monthly Recap*. Though they found writing the articles a challenge, they considered it part of their education, sort of like working for a school newspaper.

It was a great way to break the ice and approach some of the best players on the tour. They were still teenage girls, after all. Rather than work up the courage to talk with an older, established champion, they scheduled interviews for the newsletter. That allowed them the freedom to act as a reporter and ask anything they wanted. It was a chance to learn something from veterans.

One of those was Pete Sampras, who would win fourteen Grand Slam titles and was considered one of the greatest players of all time. Both girls wanted to meet him and gain advice. He was known for being shy and quiet, though. The regular tennis media always painted him as dull. By making him the feature story in *Tennis Monthly Recap*, they got a chance to talk to him and quickly developed a friendship with someone who would mentor them on becoming a champion. They also discovered a different person than the one they had read about.

"I thought Pete was boring; you guys really make it seem that way," Serena said at the time to the media. "But he's really not. He's funny. He was laughing the whole time."

The 1999 tennis season also featured the first ever all–Williams sisters final in a pro event, the Lipton Championships in Key Biscayne, Florida. As much as Richard had tried to keep them from competing against each other, at this point, there was no avoiding these matchups. Both Venus and Serena were ready for the biggest and best tournaments, and they were capable of beating anyone to get to the finals.

Venus won 6–1, 4–6, 6–4, but it was a hard-fought match. For Richard and Oracene, it was emotional. This felt like a dream come true. Richard was so overcome while watching that he thought he was going to cry. He eventually decided he couldn't bear to watch, so he got up, walked around the stadium, and went to the concession stand. It had been a long, hard, unlikely road.

"What I thought actually would be going through my mind was how happy I was to see both my girls being out there," Richard said. "What really was going through my mind was all the problems we've had in tennis, bringing the girls up, how difficult it was, all the gang members, all the people out there. I guess I was just thinking about those things. I was saying, 'Look where you are today.' It was so difficult for me to believe it."

Neither Venus nor Serena even realized their dad left. Each was too busy trying to beat the other. While many members of the media and fans wondered if two sisters could compete with the same ferocity and intensity of two unrelated opponents, Serena said that wasn't the case. As much as she and her sister loved each other, they were also competitors who hated losing.

"Especially after a little while, you want to win," Serena said. "You're thinking, 'I can win.' You're not thinking about who's actually over there . . . I looked over at her sometimes, and I didn't consider her Venus or my sister; I just considered her an opponent . . . When I'm playing someone, I don't think about who I'm playing. I'm just playing the ball. I'm not playing my opponent. Doesn't matter who I play, when I play them, where I play them."

If only fans, the media, and other players believed her.

US OPEN	CHAMPIONSHIP
Hingis	4
S. Williams	4

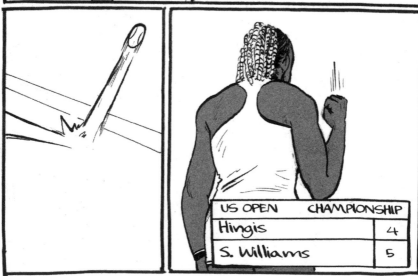

US OPEN	CHAMPIONSHIP
Hingis	4
S. Williams	5

8

Controversy

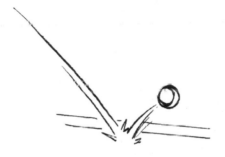

THE ALL ENGLAND Lawn Tennis and Croquet Club was founded in 1868 in Wimbledon, an area not far from Central London. Membership was exclusive and consisted, as it still does, of wealthy and high-society people. In 1877, it staged its first tennis championship, which over the years became known simply as "Wimbledon." It is the oldest, and arguably most prestigious, such tournament in the world.

The event is rooted in tradition. Players must wear all-white (or nearly all-white) uniforms. They are referred to by the public-address announcer as Mr., Miss, or Mrs. ("Game Miss Williams"), adding a level of stiffness to the event. Ball boys and girls stand at rapt attention. The most popular concession stand item isn't popcorn or nachos; it's strawberries and cream. Up until 2003, players were expected to bow or curtsy to any member of the royal family that attends the matches. (Over the years the Williams sisters even became friends with younger royals such as Kate Middleton and Prince William, and Serena attended the 2018 wedding of Meghan Markle and Prince Harry.)

The most notable tradition is that the tournament is played on grass courts, which is why it's called "lawn tennis." The grass is cut very short so the court is hard and perfectly flat. The ball tends to bounce very quickly off the surface—even faster than the hard courts used for the Australian and the US Open, and much faster than the clay courts of the French Open.

The grass, combined with the other rituals, makes Wimbledon seem more formal than any other tournament. After all, any city, club, school, or even a person in their backyard can lay an asphalt court and begin playing tennis. Very few players have ever seen a grass court, which takes enormous time and money to not just construct, but maintain on a daily basis.

All this is why Wimbledon is so important, intimidating, and beloved. The Williams sisters, who grew up watching it on television, certainly felt that way. It's what made the 2000 tournament so significant as they each worked through the competition to meet in the semifinals. This was the deepest in a Grand Slam they had ever played each other. It also assured that one of them would go on to the finals. The game would be at Centre Court. A global audience was excited to see the sisters compete in a major match. Anyone with a sibling could try to wonder how they would handle the situation. The anticipation was incredible, even as Venus and Serena tried to claim it was just another match.

"There is no sibling rivalry," Serena said. "Tennis is just a game. Family is forever."

Then the match took place and Venus won in straight sets 6–2, 7–6 (7–3 tiebreaker). Serena had entered the semifinals playing some of her best tennis, but she committed a number of unforced errors and double faults. She didn't appear as aggressive as she had been earlier in the tournament. The action was somewhat dull and anticlimactic. Serena's poor performance gave credence to the idea that she wasn't trying as hard to defeat her sister as she would if it was, say, Martina Hingis. Others even believed that Richard had told her to let Venus win.

Serena brushed it off, saying it was just a bad day against a great opponent. After all, just two days later Venus would win her first Wimbledon title by defeating Lindsay Davenport by nearly an identical score of 6–3, 7–6 (7–3), and no one suggested that Lindsay wasn't trying. Both sisters said they'd never throw a match, let alone one deep in a Grand Slam.

"It's a title on the line," Serena said years later on *Oprah*. "It's a lot of money. It's a Grand Slam that goes on the history records. I want to win, and I know Venus wants to win. It's the apex of the sport. It's what you dream about when you are younger."

Critics were not convinced. While Venus and Serena were winning and bringing in new fans to the sport, they still struggled for acceptance in some places. The doubt about how hard the sisters would compete against each other was just one example.

Tennis was, and in many ways still remains, a sport that is mostly white and mostly conservative. When Serena or Venus entered a tournament, they were often the only black players. Richard was often the only black coach. Administrators, officials, umpires, and even ball boys and girls were almost all white. So too was the crowd in the stands. But the fact that they stood out went beyond race. They both were very interested in fashion and often wore and even designed bright, colorful outfits, which were distinct from the plainer clothes most players wore. Their hair was often in beads, which especially at that time was a hairstyle worn almost exclusively by African Americans.

Some fans even complained the girls were too muscular or too powerful for the women's game. They compared them to the men's players and felt that their physiques gave them an unfair advantage. How were Venus and Serena supposed to respond to that? Their physiques were their physiques. Others tried to claim that, while they could hit the ball hard, they weren't really great all-around players. That was criticism that stung the sisters. Because, intentional or not, this type of criticism is rooted in racist views.

"A lot of people think that black people can't rally, just think they're athletes and they can't think," Serena said. "As you can see, that's not true. I can rally; Venus can rally." Others complained when Serena would shout to herself in an effort to fire up her game. She routinely clenched her fists and screamed "Come on!" to herself. It became a signature moment, but some fans criticized her for it even though doing such things is common with lots of great athletes.

Venus and Serena were having fun and being true to themselves. They always followed the rules and were respectful, but they looked and thought differently than others. That seemingly everything they did troubled someone was painful to accept. Serena tried to combat it by ignoring all the chatter and not reading or watching coverage of the sport or listening to the fans.

"I think there's a lot of new attitudes out here," Serena said. "It brings a lot of excitement to the sport . . . More people are looking at tennis. More people are realizing that tennis is actually a fun sport to play. It's exciting to watch ladies actually go out there and compete, watch ladies be pretty, watch ladies sweat."

They were also raised to consider family first. All those years together meant they hadn't come up like many other players—training, playing, and becoming friends with others on the junior circuit.

They just had each other. Richard coached no other players. And even when they were at the Rick Macci Tennis Academy, they usually practiced with older boys. There wasn't a lot of common ground or shared experiences.

While Serena and Venus always tried to be polite and nice, they were focused on winning. Like so many other great champions in sports, they were intense before matches. Some of this was a new attitude for the sport of tennis, especially women's tennis. When Venus and Serena were on the road, they stayed with each other, ate meals with each other, and practiced with each other. They spent most of their free time together or with their family. They were still playing a limited schedule due to school (Serena had to turn in an English paper back in Florida while winning that first tournament at Indian Wells). Almost no one else was still pursuing her education. All this meant that the other players on the tour didn't get to see what they were like away from competition. Some viewed them with suspicion.

"I think maybe they feel we're apart," Serena said. "I don't know . . . I communicate with other players. I smile. I'm cordial, friendly. I don't know. I'm just trying to be me."

It would all come to a head in 2001 when both

sisters reached the semifinals of the Indian Wells Masters tournament. Two years prior, Serena had won the event, her first ever Tier I title. This year, she breezed to the semis again to face Venus. However, Venus was suffering from an injured knee and struggled through her quarterfinal victory over Russian Elena Dementieva. Venus wasn't certain she'd be healthy enough to take on Serena in the semifinals.

Dementieva was asked who she thought would win the semifinal between Venus and Serena. She provided a public voice to what many were saying privately: that any match involving Venus and Serena was predetermined by their father, who would choose the winner.

"I don't know, what [does] Richard think about it?" Dementieva said. "I think he will decide who's going to win."

The idea that either Venus or Serena, two smart and hard-nosed competitors, would be compliant to their father and happily do whatever he said was highly insulting. It spoke to an ignorance about who the Williams sisters were. No matter how many times Venus and Serena denied it, people saw them as mindless robots, perhaps believing because of their skin color or upbringing that they couldn't think for themselves. The precise opposite was true, of course. However, since both of them were raised to avoid confrontation with other players, they just tried to politely brush the controversy aside rather than attack the issue.

"People have the freedom of speech," Serena said. "They can say whatever they want." That didn't mean it didn't upset her. "It's really kind of hurtful because it's just lies, just scandalous lies."

Just minutes before the semifinal match at Indian Wells, Venus pulled out due to injury. She had tried to warm up, but her knee wasn't responding. "I was moving like a grandma," Venus said. Serena had no idea. She was warming up herself, expecting to play.

Fans who had come to watch the semifinal were angry. They booed the announcement and went to the ticket office looking to get their money back. Many viewed this as a way for the Williams family to make sure Serena advanced to the finals without even having to exert herself in the semifinals. By giving Serena extra rest, they believed this amounted to cheating. They were convinced that Richard told Venus to fake the injury, even though the Williams family denied it.

"I made every effort to be on the court, stretching, warming up, taping, seeing the doctor . . . ,"

Venus said. "The truth is, I'm suffering from an injury."

The fans at Indian Wells were not satisfied with that answer. Two days later, Serena was set to play Kim Clijsters in the finals. As Serena walked onto the court for the match, she was greeted by waves of boos and jeers from some of the fifteen thousand fans in attendance. There was even more booing and shouting when Richard and Venus walked down to their seats in the grandstands to watch and cheer on Serena. Richard said he heard racial taunts, and he turned to the crowd and held his fist aloft, which is a sign that symbolizes pride and solidarity among black people. Everything got even more heated. Serena said she heard racial slurs and the n-word and was told to "go back to Compton."

"I couldn't believe it," Serena wrote. "That's just not something you hear in polite society."

When Kim Clijsters, who is white, took the court, the crowd cheered for her. Kim was seventeen, a young and popular player. It wasn't uncommon for fans to cheer for her. She and Serena were friends. Kim grew up in Belgium, though. Serena was from California, playing in front of Californian fans in California. This was an event Serena had won before. She considered it a special place and had always praised the city, the organizers, and the fans. Yet they were against her and for Kim. Serena was now well aware that even though it was Venus who'd pulled out of the tournament, she was the villain in this match. Everything was coming to a head.

"It was a very tense situation," the announcer on ESPN remarked on the air that night. "I've never seen anything like this at a tennis match."

When they started playing, the crowd was loud and intimidating. When Serena double faulted, people roared in approval. When Kim drilled a winner down the line, they stood and applauded. When Serena made a good shot, it wasn't completely silent, but it was noticeably quieter.

"I don't think I was mentally ready for that," Serena said. "I don't think I was mentally ready for that at all."

Many fans *were* there to watch tennis and didn't choose a side. They cheered for both players. And there were other people there cheering for Serena. Not everyone there was motivated by racism or the belief that the Williams family was cheating the system and choosing the winners. Some were, though. And they were making their allegiance and opinion known. Serena was rattled. Kim Clijsters took the first set 6–4. Some of the crowd went wild.

"I mean, how many people do you know go out there and jeer a nineteen-year-old?" Serena said. "Come on, I'm just a kid."

During a break, Serena sat down and fell back on her faith to carry her through what she felt was a "chaotic" situation. "I prayed to God just to help me be strong, not even to win, but to be strong, not listen to the crowd . . . I just wanted some strength to go on."

Feeling more relaxed, Serena slowly found her game. She realized the quickest way to silence the crowd was to hit winning shots. Some of her fans even began to get more vocal and cheer her on. Others were just amazed at her ability. She won the second set 6–4 and then took the championship by winning the third 6–2. Serena was most proud that she had the mental toughness to rally and win in such a hostile, difficult, and insensitive environment.

"I have to believe there was some racist component to it," Serena wrote years later. "Nobody would have booed some blond, blue-eyed girl."

There was a post-match celebration that included a smattering of more boos. It was awkward. They presented Serena with a trophy and a microphone. She didn't know what to say to the fans who had just treated her so poorly and unfairly. She would soon break down in tears as she drove back to Los Angeles. She would be haunted by the experience, now suspicious of fans everywhere. She would vow to never return to Indian Wells. Both Serena and Venus boycotted the tournament for years, even as the WTA fined them for skipping the event. At that moment, though, she didn't want to make a big deal about it and allow the fans to see that they had gotten to her.

"You guys were a little tough on me today," Serena said. "I'd like to thank everyone who supported me. And if you didn't, I love you guys anyway."

She then grabbed a ceremonial check that they give to the champion made out for $330,000 and left. Racism, ignorance, and suspicions weren't going to stop Serena Williams. Not then. Not ever.

9

Serena Slam

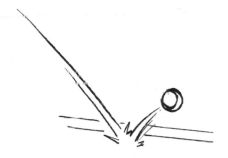

THE UPROAR AFTER Indian Wells did not die
down quickly. But Serena took one positive from
the event: She now knew she was mentally tough
enough to handle any situation that tennis could
throw at her. Nothing would be as intimidating as
that, not even a Grand Slam final standing across
the court from Martina Hingis, Steffi Graf, or her
sister Venus, who had won Wimbledon and the US
Open in both 2000 and 2001. That would just be
tennis. If she could win at Indian Wells with the fans
booing her, she could do anything.

Serena focused on what she called the "Mind-set of a Champion." She came to believe that champions act a certain way and that this, in turn, brings about championships. It includes little things, like always focusing on diet, stretching, sleep habits, and other behavior, even weeks before a tournament.

It also requires maintaining the killer instinct to close out matches when the opportunity arises. And it requires remaining confident that you can handle difficult situations. It was Venus who gave Serena some simple advice: "A champion in tight situations is able to pull through," Venus told Serena. "They don't get nervous." Serena began to stay relaxed, even under pressure, the way she did at Indian Wells.

"You have to take things as they come," Serena said. "Things don't always go your way. I think in the past I wanted things to go my way too often, but I was able to change that and realize if I was in this situation, what would I do?"

Her growth and maturity as a player was on display at the 2001 US Open. Serena's goal that year was to win multiple Grand Slams, but it didn't work out. She lost in the quarterfinals of the Australian Open, French Open, and Wimbledon. Little was expected of Serena as she entered the US Open. She was seeded tenth, an afterthought behind Martina Hingis and Jennifer Capriati, who had returned to the tour after personal problems and was again a great player. Then there was, of course, Venus.

Serena dropped the first set of her first match to unseeded underdog Anca Barna, who had never in her career cracked the top 100 in the rankings. Rather than collapse, though, Serena leaned on the Mind-set of a Champion and just focused on playing her game. She wouldn't let the last point cost her the next point. She won the next two sets and the match. Then she started rolling, winning match after match, until she reached the semifinals.

Against top-seed Martina Hingis, Serena was brilliant, winning 6–3, 6–2. Her serve was simply overwhelming. In the second set, she never missed on her first serve, placing fast, accurate shot after fast, accurate shot. "I can't serve any better than that," Serena said. Martina Hingis had no chance.

Serena's serve had gone from great to perhaps the greatest of all time in women's tennis. It turned her into a very dangerous opponent. She had three key advantages. First was her power. On a first serve, a player can risk faulting and really smash it, since they'll have a second opportunity if needed.

Serena's serve velocity would routinely hit more than 120 miles per hour, which is very difficult to even get a racket on to return. Second, she enjoyed incredible placement of her shot, almost always on the edges of the service box, forcing opponents to reach just to get to the ball. Third, thanks to the training she began with her dad as a kid, she was a master at tossing the ball in a way that her opponent couldn't figure out which way she was hitting it—to the middle or the edge. That left almost no reaction time. When her serve was on, she was almost impossible to beat.

"I couldn't read her serve," a frustrated Hingis said. "I didn't know whether she was going forehand or backhand. She was hitting the lines and the corners. It was difficult to even reach it. Even [when] I got there, there's not much I could do with it."

But for Serena, advancing to the final was a little bittersweet because once again she'd be facing off against her best friend and sister. Venus and Serena's first Grand Slam final matchup was another highly anticipated match for fans. Both were playing magnificent tennis. Numerous celebrities came out to watch and TV ratings around America soared. There was no backlash or booing like there was at Indian Wells. Serena felt the crowd was split between the two sisters—"I think maybe the older sisters and older brothers wanted Venus to win," Serena said. "The younger sisters and younger brothers wanted me to win."

If so, the older siblings went home happy. Venus won 6–2, 6–4. She was simply too good. Her record against her younger sister went to 5–1 overall (not counting the withdrawal at Indian Wells).

Serena wasn't too frustrated, though. "I think she's beaten everyone," Serena said. Serena saw a bright side to the strong tournament. Her game was getting sharp. Her confidence was skyrocketing. And her serve was simply vicious. She could sense that her time was coming.

It turned out it was coming quickly. In 2002, Serena began to dominate the tennis world, including her sister.

A sprained ankle kept her out of the Australian Open, but she went to the French open and won her second career Grand Slam by defeating Venus in straight sets in the finals. Then she went to Wimbledon and did it again, beating two-time defending champion Venus 7–6 (7–4), 6–3. Serena was so dominant, she didn't lose a single set the entire tournament! Serena was thrilled to win Wimbledon in part because singles champions are given a lifetime membership in the All England Lawn Tennis and Croquet Club. They are even presented a membership pin.

"I just wanted Wimbledon," Serena said. "I wanted to become a member of so much prestige, so much history. I want to be a part of history."

She wasn't done with the year, either. At the US Open, she won again and once more it was against Venus in the finals. Just like at Wimbledon, she didn't drop a set the entire tournament. No one could hang with her, certainly not when her service was on. Serena entered thirteen tournaments in 2002, reached ten finals, and won eight championships. She went 56–5 overall in matches. It was an incredible run. She won every Grand Slam match she played in—finishing 21–0. Serena said it was as much due to her new mind-set as to any development to her game.

"I was just tired of losing," Serena said. "It's not that I thought I could win all three [Grand Slams]. I just said, 'I'm tired of losing. I'm not going to lose anymore' . . . You know, [there] comes a point in one's life where they get tired, whether it's with losing or with whatever the case may be. At this point I was tired. Life was passing me by."

Such an incredible year pushed Serena to number one in the world rankings, unseating Venus, who was knocked down to second. They had combined to win five of the last six Grand Slams, facing off against each other in all but one of them. They had also teamed up to win five Grand Slam doubles titles. Then there were the 2000 Olympics in Sydney, Australia, where, competing for Team USA, Venus won the gold medal in singles, and she and Serena took home the gold in doubles. There was no denying that the Williams sisters' control over women's tennis, just the way Richard long ago envisioned it, was complete.

About the only disappointment was that Serena hadn't won all four Grand Slams in 2002. The "Calendar Slam" is when a player wins them all in the same year. Only five singles players have ever accomplished this. Since Serena hadn't even competed in the 2002 Australian Open, which is played each January, she never really had a chance. She was already eyeing the 2003 Australian, though. Winning there would make her the reigning champion of all four Grand Slams. She decided to come up with her own term for such an accomplishment.

"It's a Serena Slam," she said.

The quest for the Serena Slam reached the Australian semifinals and then found its greatest challenge, Kim Clijsters. Serena and Kim split the first two sets, but then Kim took a 5–1 lead in the deciding third set. Serena meanwhile was suffering from multiple blisters on her foot, making it difficult to move. Once again, Serena went back to the Mindset of a Champion. Rather than worry about what went wrong to cause her to fall so far behind in the match, she thought about what she could do right on the next swing, the next point. She had come too far in an attempt to win all four Grand Slams to give up without a fight.

"I don't go out there thinking, 'Gosh, I'm going to lose,'" Serena said. "I don't care if I'm down 6–Love, 5–Love, Love–40. I always think positively out there. [I] always say, 'Let me try a little harder, try a little harder. Just go for one point, just this point.'"

Facing elimination, Serena won the next game. In the following game, Kim Clijsters was serving and quickly went up 40–30. She was one point away from winning the match when Serena hammered a return shot that Kim couldn't handle and forced deuce. A couple of points later, Kim again served for the match. Serena fought that one off, too, and took the game. It was now 5–3. Serena held serve to make it 5–4. Kim was clearly nervous. Despite holding the lead and the serve, she came undone. Kim couldn't deliver the shots she had been delivering all day long. She twice double faulted, and Serena pounced to even the set at 5–5. With Kim reeling, Serena took the next two games and finished off one of her greatest comebacks, 7–5, to advance to the finals.

"It was just an unbelievable battle out there," Serena said.

"I could feel that she was really trying to step it up, and that she was, you know, hitting the balls a lot more aggressive and had almost [no] unforced errors at the end," Clijsters said. "That's when you just have to say, 'too good.' You know, that's why she's the number one."

After the incredible comeback, Venus once again was waiting in the finals. After three consecutive defeats, Venus was determined to beat her younger sister. It showed. The match was intense. Venus and Serena took turns blasting powerful shots and brilliant winners at each other. The energy that they put into the game thrilled fans around the world. Absolutely no one could suggest that this match was predetermined or that Venus wasn't trying her hardest. It was a battle.

In the end, Serena won again, 7–6 (7–4), 3–6, 6–4. It extended her victory streak over Venus to four, all of them in a Grand Slam final. If not for Serena, it's possible Venus would have won each of those championships. Instead, she had to settle for being the second-best player not only in the world, but in her own family.

"I think right now she's just probably a little mentally tougher," Venus said. "They are not fun to lose."

For Serena, owning all four Grand Slams at the same time was almost unimaginable. At that moment, no other woman owned a reigning Grand Slam trophy. Her streak would end that year when Justine Henin-Hardenne upset her 6–2, 4–6, 7–5 in the French Open semifinals. It ended Serena's remarkable thirty-three-match Grand Slam winning streak. She then proved her ability to bounce back that summer at Wimbledon, winning the championship again, and again defeating Venus in the finals to do it.

Serena was just twenty-one years old but already owned six Grand Slam titles, including the Serena

Slam. She had been number one in the world. She had endorsement deals, money, fame, and talent. Mostly, though, she knew that the accomplishments on the court would put her down in history as one of the greatest tennis players ever.

The question was whether she wanted to be *the* greatest.

OUT!

Serena wins!

US OPEN	CHAMPIONSHIP		
Hingis		3	6
S. Williams		6	7

ARTHUR ASHE STADIUM

10

Tragedy

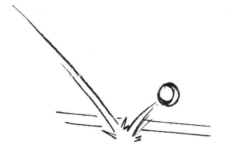

AFTER WIMBLEDON, SERENA returned to Los Angeles. One night, she and some friends decided to go out dancing to celebrate her championship. It was then, at a nightclub, that she injured her knee . . . dancing. Yes, one of the finest athletes in the world was injured not from chasing down a ball at the US Open or through the brutal repetition of practice, but, of all things, from dancing with her friends.

The lesson? "Don't dance in heels," Serena would joke.

The knee would need surgery and time to rehab. It sidelined Serena at a point when her game was at peak performance. That was frustrating. It did allow her some time to pursue other passions. She continued with college. She worked with Puma on designing clothes. And she took a brief role as an actress in a cable television drama.

On September 14, 2003, Serena was in Toronto for filming when her phone rang early in the morning. It was her mother, Oracene, asking if she had heard from Yetunde, Serena's oldest sister. Yetunde was thirty-one at the time and still lived in LA. Her mother said that Yetunde hadn't come home from a night out, no one knew where she was, and she wasn't answering her phone. Serena immediately became worried.

Serena and Yetunde had spent lots of hours together recently since Serena was temporarily living in LA while rehabbing her knee. She had always loved Yetunde, who as the oldest of the sisters was protective, nurturing, caring, and a lot of fun to be around. Yetunde had become a registered nurse and an owner of a beauty salon near where the Williamses were raised in Compton. She was the mother of three children. She sometimes worked as an assistant for Venus and Serena and often traveled to their biggest matches, cheering them on in the family box.

Serena hung up and called Yetunde's house. A cousin answered and delivered the shocking news— Yetunde was gone. She had been killed that night in a shooting. Serena couldn't believe what she was hearing. She had just been with Yetunde before going to Toronto. Their sister Lyndrea was staying with Serena and helping her out on the road. The two were sharing a hotel room, and upon hearing the news, immediately collapsed in confusion, grief, and anger.

Yetunde had gone out to dinner the previous night with some friends. After dinner, they were driving through Compton less than two miles from the corner tennis courts where the family learned the game. That's when they drove by a house that a local gang used to sell drugs. As they passed by, one of the gang members pulled out a gun and shot at the SUV, perhaps out of mistaken identity. Yetunde died soon after being taken to a local hospital.

The pain and horror were incalculable. Everyone understood that the dangers of Compton were not just that you could easily be swept up by gangs or drugs as a child. It was also that even innocent people can get caught in the crossfire and lose their lives through senseless violence. By Venus and Serena becoming rich and famous tennis stars, there was a belief that their family had survived the old neighborhood. This was proof they hadn't. Those bullets didn't care that Yetunde was a nurse and a business owner, and an educated, self-made woman and a devoted mother to three children who needed her. Those bullets didn't care how many Grand Slam titles her two younger sisters had won.

All they did was bring tragedy to the Williams family.

The next weeks and months were a blur for Serena and her family. Oracene moved into Yetunde's house in nearby Carson, California, and began raising the children as her own. The family came together to mourn and support one another. It had already been a confusing time for Serena, because in 2002 her parents divorced. While she was a grown-up herself now, it was still a disappointment, a shock, and a big change. She had to adjust to having a mom and dad who were separated. She had to accept that while things would never be the same, or how she wanted, life could still be good. The Williamses' reaction following Yetunde's death reminded her how tight her family still was.

Serena needed to continue to rehab but did so in a daze, weighed down by a heavy heart. The gunman was arrested and eventually pleaded guilty to manslaughter. He had never met Yetunde and wasn't shooting at her. He just shot the SUV. She was in the wrong place at the wrong time.

At the sentencing hearing where the judge sent the gunman to prison, Serena overcame her emotions and spoke directly to her sister's killer. She wanted to convey her family's sadness, rage, and frustration. Serena reminded him that they had always represented Compton in a positive light, always given back to the community, always tried to tell people around the country and the world about all the good people who lived there. And yet, he did this to them.

"This was unfair to our family," Serena said, looking the killer in the eyes. "Our family has always been positive, and we always try to help people."

All Serena and her family could do was lean on memories: memories of those long afternoons playing tennis at the "Compton Hills Country Club"; of squeezing five sisters into two bunk beds in one room; of the kitchen-table card games and living-room dance contests; and of the trips to London and Paris to experience Grand Slams together.

One thing Serena always appreciated was how supportive Yetunde was of Venus and her. There was never any jealousy at their accomplishments. Yetunde lived her own life and had her own success. She was more than just the older sister to two famous tennis players. She was proud, too. "She was so happy for me and Venus," Serena said. Yetunde was either the one cheering the loudest in the family courtside box or one of the first on the phone to congratulate her.

Serena had a habit of writing notes to herself that she would pull out and read during breaks in matches. She had found that she was easily distracted. While resting for a minute, Serena would let her mind wander or begin looking around the stadium. When play resumed, she'd sometimes give away a few points or even a game before she refocused. The little notes with simple reminders about her game were part of her Mind-set of a Champion.

"Usually I write, 'Look at the ball, move forward, do this, do that,'" Serena said. "Just things that I need to work on."

After Yetunde's murder, she sometimes brought a single note with a single word. "Just 'Yetunde,'" Serena said at the 2007 Australian Open. "That was all my notes. That's it. Every changeover I looked at it, and I just thought about how happy she would have been, how much she always supported me. I just thought about what an amazing sister she was to me. I just said, 'Serena, this has to be motivating. This has to be more than enough to motivate.'"

One thing the Williams family didn't want was for Yetunde's murder to end their ties to their hometown. While it took years before they could manage to return to Compton, they didn't abandon it in anger and anguish. Instead, they decided to redouble their efforts to help the people who live there. These were people they lived next to, grew up with, and understood. They knew the struggles. They knew the fears. They knew what was needed. Through the Williams Sisters Fund, a charity that Venus and Serena ran, they later opened the Yetunde Price Resource Center. It works with area schools and law enforcement to teach violence prevention by reaching out to at-risk kids. It also provides support and counseling for victims of violence. It opened on Compton Boulevard, not far from their old home.

"People are able to get support, and understand what government programs or grants are available for them," Serena said. "[There's] psychological support, therapy through art. We are supporting families and helping them pick up the pieces, but of course a lot of work to be done in prevention, as well."

The city of Compton did its part to honor its famous former residents by refurbishing a park in the city. It added a couple of new, and much-needed, tennis courts. At a big ceremony, they were named the Venus & Serena Williams Court of Champions.

"We're really appreciative," Serena said. "To have it in Compton, I think, brings everything full circle. We started here, and we want to make sure people understand this is a great place to be."

Through triumph and tragedy, Serena's connection to her hometown remained.

11

Depression

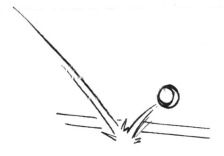

RETURNING TO THE COURT was not easy for Serena. Her knee needed continued rehab. Her distress over the murder of her sister carried on. Tennis just didn't matter much to her. She was eventually capable of physically returning but not at the elite level needed to win Grand Slams or push for number one in the world.

In 2004, she entered twelve tournaments and won just two, a low ratio for her. None were Grand Slams. In 2005, she entered ten and won just one;

albeit it was the Australian Open for her eighth Grand Slam. She never got through the quarter-finals in the other three major tournaments. In 2006, injuries and other issues limited her to just four events and zero victories. She slipped all the way to ninety-five in the world rankings. There was another Grand Slam title in 2007 at the Australian Open but little else. It was the same for most of 2008.

Serena was still a good player, capable of being the best in the world on any given day. As she cruised through her twenties, however, there were questions about whether her career was on a downward slide. Was she burned out like so many other tennis prodigies? Had she lost the hunger to compete at the highest level? Were the injuries keeping her from being in tip-top physical condition? Was she just a step slow now as she grew "old" by tennis standards?

What Serena was suffering from, she later realized and acknowledged, was depression. It may not seem possible for someone with so many trophies, so many millions of dollars, so many fans to be depressed, but how someone feels internally rarely has anything to do with how they are viewed externally. She was still winning some tournaments, even an occasional Grand Slam, but that was just her physical self mostly going through the motions. That nearly everyone else in the world would have gladly changed positions with Serena Williams didn't matter either. She felt how she felt.

"It was an aching sadness, an all-over weariness, a sudden disinterest in the world around me—in tennis, above all," Serena would later write. Injuries that piled up were good excuses to take a break, but until she confronted the reality of her feelings, nothing would be resolved. It didn't help that she wasn't discussing anything with her mother, her father, or any of her sisters, even Venus. She kept it bottled up.

"I wasn't honest with myself about how I was feeling, what I was thinking," Serena wrote. "I'd never been honest with stuff like this—and that right there was the root of my troubles."

Eventually she began to confront her truth. She fell back on her faith. She realized that until she was content with herself, nothing else mattered. Finding internal peace had to be a priority. She tried to stop worrying about all the people who relied on her and all the fans who expected perfection from her. Instead, she sought a calm, fulfilling, consistent, and spiritual life. She read. She meditated. She went to counseling. She traveled to Africa twice. She slowly found herself.

"I started seeing a therapist," Serena wrote. "The more I talked the more I realized that my gloomy funk had to do with making people happy. It came up because of [Yetunde]. It came up because of me not playing following my knee injury . . . it came up because of all those weeks at number one, and the pressures I felt to get back there. It was all these things, but the main ingredient was me trying to please everyone else."

In the process, she also discovered that she loved tennis. When she wasn't playing, she missed it. Not just the competition or the cheering crowds or the satisfaction of winning. She missed the actual game of tennis. The shots. The serves. The running. The strategy.

She hadn't chosen the sport as a kid. It had been chosen for her. Richard Williams had said she would be a champion before she was even born. She poured her life into it, and it returned incredible rewards, but whether or not she truly loved tennis remained a question. Without that love of the game, her career would likely end. She already had plenty of money. She didn't need to play. As athletes get older and all the wear and tear of the games and practices ravage the body, it can feel more and more like a job. Suddenly, at age twenty-seven, Serena began to see it as more of a game.

She found herself looking forward to practice. There were days she'd get out of bed before dawn, eager to work. She'd head to the court and then realize it was still dark. "I would have to wait until it got light," Serena said. With that renewed ambition, her game began to return. She played thirteen events in 2008, the most since 2002. She won four, the most since 2003.

She entered Wimbledon that year seeded sixth and stormed to the finals, where she ran into a familiar foe—Venus. This time, the older sister denied her younger sister a Grand Slam with a score of 7–5, 6–4.

There was something to build on, though. At the US Open, Serena was unbeatable, never dropping a single set (her toughest match was against Venus in the quarterfinals). In winning her ninth Grand Slam, she again earned the top ranking in the world. She was back, and in many ways, better (or more at peace with herself) than ever.

"I feel like I have a new career, like I feel so

young and I feel so energized to play every week and to play every tournament," Serena said after winning the 2008 US Open. "I feel like there's just so much that I can do in my career yet, and I've never felt like I've played my best tennis."

In 2009, she won both the Australian Open and Wimbledon, her tenth and eleventh Grand Slam titles. At Wimbledon, she defeated Venus in the finals 7–6 (7–3), 6–2. It was a straight sets victory, but it was extremely competitive.

The victory was particularly notable because it made Serena's record against Venus 11–10, marking the first time Serena had more wins head-to-head against her sister. It was a career lead she would never relinquish. It further cemented the younger as better than the elder.

The action was fierce, but there was no bitterness to the rivalry. Just a couple of hours after Serena defeated Venus in the singles final, the two teamed up in the finals of the doubles tournament. This occasionally happened during their career, going from opponents to teammates in a matter of hours. The sisters had come up with a system—don't discuss the singles match that had just occurred. After all, while one would be happy, the other would be sad. Rather, they would act like it didn't happen and just focus on winning in doubles. It worked at Wimbledon as Venus and Serena took home their ninth doubles Grand Slam title. Not a bad day at work for Serena Williams.

"You can go home with two titles," Serena said. "There's nothing like winning a title with your sister."

Serena was again on top of the tennis world. Her endorsement deals with giant brands like Nike, Gatorade, and Delta Airlines led to advertisements that put her face everywhere, even when she wasn't playing tennis. In 2009, she and Venus bought shares of the NFL Miami Dolphins, making them the first African American women to ever own part of a major pro football franchise. Serena was a regular in pop culture—from acting to cameos in music videos.

Most important, however, Serena increased her charitable work. Through her foundation, she funded college scholarships to kids across America. She also opened the Serena Williams Secondary School in Kenya, offering educational opportunities to the children she met during numerous trips to Africa. She got one of her business partners,

Hewlett-Packard, to donate all the computers. She insisted that at least 40 percent of the students were female, an important and empowering act in a part of the world where girls were often treated as inferior. A few years later, she opened a second school.

"That's better than holding up [a] trophy . . . ," Serena said. "You see these people who are living souls who you actually are helping to learn, help get an education, which can ameliorate their country. I feel like for me [opening the school] was the most wonderful moment in my career."

In 2010, the success continued. She would turn twenty-nine that year, but her five-foot-nine frame was still an ideal combination of agility and power. Only now she truly knew how to play in any situation. "I feel like I'm a little bit of a better player because I'm more experienced now, and I know more what to do and I know how to play the tough moments," Serena said.

She again won the Australian Open and Wimbledon, pushing her to thirteen Grand Slams, one better than her one-time idol Billie Jean King. The media began speculating that she might be able to pass legends Martina Navratilova and Chris Evert, who had won eighteen, or even Steffi Graf, with twenty-two. Serena didn't know what to think. She was again happy and healthy, and that's what mattered most. She kept claiming that how many Grand Slams she eventually won didn't matter.

"I'm telling you, I don't think about that kind of stuff," Serena said. "My thing is I love my dogs; I love my family; I love going to the movies; I love reading; I love going shopping . . . At the end of the day, I would love to open more schools in Africa or in the United States, and I would love to help people. I would like to be remembered, 'Okay, yeah, she was a tennis player, but wow, she really did a lot to inspire other people and help other people.' That's what I think about, not about 'Serena Williams won X amount of Grand Slams.'"

12

Dominance

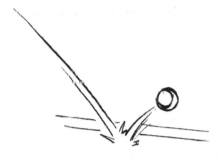

FOUR DAYS AFTER SERENA won the 2010 Wimbledon championship, she was at a restaurant in Germany. She went with some of her family to celebrate and enjoy a vacation. After dinner, while wearing sandals, she walked out only to realize that she had stepped on some broken glass, cutting both of her feet. She received eighteen stitches. When she got back to the United States, she realized that her feet didn't just hurt from the cuts. Her big toe wasn't working as it normally did. Instead it drooped.

Doctors diagnosed a torn tendon. This was the second time a freak injury had occurred after Wimbledon. Serena had surgery to fix it and missed the 2010 US Open and the 2011 Australian Open.

Things only got worse from there. In February 2011, Serena was rushed to the hospital suffering from blood clots in her lungs, which if left untreated or undetected could have been fatal. Surgery removed the blood clots, but blood-thinning medicine designed to keep them from returning caused blood to build up near her stomach. That required another surgery and more time to try to regain her health. During long stints in the hospital, Serena was surrounded by her family, some of whom would stay all night, sleeping in chairs in her room.

Altogether, Serena spent eleven months away from competition, crushing the momentum that she'd had after the Wimbledon title. She was also about to turn thirty, an age when most tennis players struggle to remain competitive at the championship level. Her comeback was difficult, and progress was slow. There were times when she didn't know if she could play again, or even if she wanted to try to play again.

"There was a moment I just remember I was on

the couch, and I didn't leave the whole day, for two days," Serena said. "I was just over it. I was praying, like, 'I can't take any more. I've endured enough. Let me be able to get through this' . . . I was just so tired at that point. I had a tube in my stomach, and it was draining constantly. Gosh, I mean, right before that I had the blood clot. I had lung problems. Then I had two foot surgeries. It was a lot. I felt like I didn't do anything to bring on that. I just felt down, the lowest of lows."

Serena said she prayed a lot. She relied on her family to lift her spirits. And she decided this was just another test for her to pass. That day on the couch was a low point, but she vowed it would be a low point she'd bounce back from.

"You know, I got up," Serena said. "I didn't just stay there. I got up. That's what you got to do sometimes. You pray and pray. I'm a pretty spiritual individual, so I'm always praying. I rely on Jehovah to give me strength. I definitely couldn't have done it without my faith. I got up, and I started."

She failed to win a Grand Slam in 2011 but began playing well in the first half of 2012. Then, just when she thought she might be returning to form, she was shockingly upset in the first round of the

French Open by Virginie Razzano, who was ranked 111th in the world. It was the only time Serena ever lost in the first round of a Grand Slam.

Serena felt something needed to change. She wasn't sharp enough. She wasn't consistent enough. She was wasting her time, and everyone else's time, if she was going lose in the first round like this.

She decided to hire a new coach. Her father, Richard, was, and remained, her coach, but he was seventy years old at that point, had gotten remarried, and was busy with a host of things. He was no longer physically able to devote endless hours to training. Serena felt she could use a new perspective, perhaps some new methods or maybe just a new voice offering advice. By getting knocked out of the French Open so quickly, she suddenly had a couple of free weeks to practice. Since Serena owned a home in Paris, she decided to stick around and work with Patrick Mouratoglou, a Frenchman who had run an elite tennis academy since 1996.

Patrick believed that Serena was fully recovered from her injuries and surgeries and that her game was more than good enough to win again. Patrick just wasn't sure Serena believed that. His strategy was to get Serena to focus on the game and not her injuries. If she could find steadiness in practice, then it would translate to matches. And if he could get her to come up with a game plan for how she was going to win the match before it was played, she could have something to fall back on when things got challenging.

"There's some times when a player doesn't believe in themselves," Serena said. "Even me. I feel like, 'Gosh, I'm not going to be able to beat this person. I'm not going to be able to play well. I don't feel confident in this shot today, I don't feel confident in that' . . .

"I think Patrick brought a lot of consistency to my game, a lot of motivation, a lot of strategy," Serena said. "I go into a match knowing exactly what to expect, what to do. It makes my life a lot easier. The motivation is really unbelievable that he has. We're a lot alike. He's a perfectionist. I'm a perfectionist. So, when I'm not where I need to be, he is there. He's like, 'You have to be better. There's no other option but to be better.'"

Almost immediately, Serena rediscovered her greatness. She had to fight through the field at Wimbledon, but she reached the finals and defeated Agnieszka Radwanska 6–1, 5–7, 6–2. It was like day and night from the French Open. Then hours later, she and Venus won the doubles title. There were no more doubts about Serena Williams. The surgeries, the blood clots, the hospital stays, and the first-round defeat were suddenly distant memories. Her serve appeared stronger than ever. The tennis world was in awe.

"It's the beginning of a great phase," Serena predicted. "I feel amazing out there. This whole tournament I felt really great physically. So I think it's definitely the beginning of something great. I hope it is."

A little over a month later, Serena was back at Wimbledon, this time competing in the 2012 Olympics in London. The Olympics were using the All England Lawn Tennis and Croquet Club as its tennis venue, which suited Serena fine. She had just won there for the fifth time. "I think my game is really suited for the grass," Serena said.

This was Serena's third Olympics. She and Venus had won the gold medal in doubles in their previous two competitions. Venus won singles gold in 2000. Now in 2012, Serena was determined to equal her sister and win her first gold in the singles competition. Growing up, both Serena and Venus loved watching the Olympics. It was what had inspired Serena to try gymnastics. She thought she might one day reach the Olympics in that sport, at least until she grew too tall. Even with all the Grand Slam titles, winning gold for Team USA meant everything.

At the Olympics, Serena was unstoppable. As tremendously as she often plays at Wimbledon, at the Olympics she was even better. In Serena's six matches, she not only won every set, but in those twelve sets, she dropped just seventeen games. It was near-perfect tennis. She was so dominant, she annihilated Maria Sharapova in the finals 6–0, 6–1, treating one of the all-time greats like a first-round weakling.

"She's playing incredibly confident tennis," Sharapova said.

Some of that, Serena acknowledged, was her new coach helping her find her old Mind-set of a Champion. "He's helped me a great deal," Serena said.

With that, Serena was on fire. She won the 2012 US Open and despite the time away from the game finished the year ranked third in the world. In 2013, she would reclaim number one and win both the French and US Opens. She entered sixteen tournaments that year and reached an astonishing thirteen finals, winning eleven titles. She went 78–4 for the year, taking 95 percent of her matches. In 2014, she won seven more individual titles, including the US Open, her eighteenth Grand Slam, tying her with Martina Navratilova and Chris Evert. She was now indisputably among the greatest players, if not the greatest, of all time.

"I just could never have imagined that I would be mentioned with Chris Evert or with Martina Navratilova because I was just a kid with a dream and a racket," Serena said. "Living in Compton, you know, this never happened before."

Steffi Graf's twenty-two Grand Slams during the so-called "Open Era" remained the record. Serena wanted to break it, but she knew the only way to do that was one point, one game, one match, and one Grand Slam at a time. With her new coach and her old health, it was just a matter of time.

She opened 2015 with a victory in Australia. Then she followed that up with another victory in France. Finally, she defeated Garbiñe Muguruza in straight sets to win Wimbledon. That gave her twenty-one Grand Slam titles. Since she also won the 2014 US Open, she now had ownership of four Slams in a row. She now had a second career "Serena Slam."

"I've been trying to win four in a row for twelve years, and it hasn't happened," Serena said. "I've had a couple injuries. You know, it's been an up-and-down process. I honestly can't say that last year or two years ago or even five years ago I wouldn't have thought that I would win four in a row. So just starting this journey, having all four trophies at home, is incredible."

The bid for the Calendar Grand Slam, however, fell apart at the US Open when Serena was upset by Italy's Roberta Vinci. It was a frustrating defeat because Serena knew how rare it was to have a chance to win all four Slams in a calendar year. Since she was about to turn thirty-four and was already the oldest woman to ever win a Grand Slam, it might've been her last chance.

There was something else notable about 2015, too. Back in March, Serena had contemplated ending her thirteen-year boycott of the WTA Tour event at Indian Wells, where she had been booed by the crowd and endured racial slurs. What happened there in 2001 remained burned into her memory. However, she had recently read a book and begun studying about the life of Nelson Mandela, a black man who was imprisoned for twenty-seven years by the white-controlled government of South Africa for his activism seeking equal rights. Upon his release, he inspired the world by offering forgiveness and peacefully negotiating with the government. He won a Nobel Prize and eventually became president of South Africa.

Serena saw parallels, albeit on a far smaller scale. The world was different. The WTA was different. The fans were different. Serena said that while she would never forget being booed and racially taunted on the court that day, she also wanted "forgiveness" to be part of the story. In order to return, she would partner with the Equal Justice Initiative, a group in Alabama that offers legal services for the poor and the imprisoned. She wanted something positive to come out of this. It had to be about more than just tennis.

"In order to forgive you have to be able to really let go of everything," Serena said. "I kind of did that a long time ago, but I still wasn't at a point where I was ready to come back to Indian Wells. I was a little nervous as well. I went through something that wasn't the best thing for me."

The decision wasn't easy. Serena knew it would

dredge up memories not just in her, but in her entire family. Her sister and father were booed and shouted at, also. Richard was accused of fixing matches. Venus was considered nothing but a puppet. Before the decision, she asked everyone what they thought. Venus wasn't ready to return. She felt she had moved on by not playing. (Venus would return in 2016 and even reached the semifinals in 2018.) Richard, meanwhile, understood the forgiveness concept right away, and while he also didn't want to go to Indian Wells, he thought Serena should.

"It would be a big mistake if you don't go back," Richard told Serena.

"I thought that was really admirable," Serena said.

It was an emotional trip. Fourteen years after being heckled off the court, Serena walked back out for her opening-round match. She was greeted by thundering applause and a standing ovation. The fans were excited to see her and thankful that forgiveness had been offered. They held signs that read WELCOME SERENA and SERENA, U R LOVED!! The reaction was incredible. Everyone wanted this to be a new day. "I heard so many people say, 'I love you, Serena,'" she said. Serena began to cry as she walked across the court, her tennis bag slung over her shoulder. "I don't think I have ever been like that." The more tears that came, the more the fans cheered and the louder the love got.

"I think they were tears of overwhelmed . . . they were just overwhelming," Serena said. "At that moment, I just felt so good to be out there. I felt like I made the right decision, and I knew I wanted to do it. I knew I really wanted to do it."

She would win her first match and progress all the way to the semifinals before a knee injury forced her to withdraw. She took the court and addressed the crowd, and this time they just cheered. There was no one questioning her will to win anymore. Besides, Serena promised to return every year.

Even in a year when she would go 53–3 overall, remain number one for all fifty-two weeks, and win three Grand Slams to run her career tally to twenty-one, putting her one win away from tying the record, she would later tell *Sports Illustrated* returning to Indian Wells was "my greatest moment in tennis."

13

Grand Slam

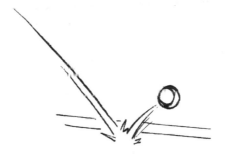

THE TENNIS WORLD was now completely obsessed with Serena's chase of Steffi Graf's record. Each event took on greater urgency, especially as Serena advanced in age. To break Steffi's record, she'd have to break her own record (twice) as the oldest woman to win a Grand Slam.

Serena said she felt better than ever, but she also found her body needed more rest days. Once-minor bumps and bruises tended to linger. The challenge would be considerable. There were also a host of young contenders, women in their early twenties, who grew up watching Serena and dreaming of beating her.

Serena reached the 2016 Australian finals but then ran into Angelique Kerber, who won a thrilling three-set match. Kerber played so well that Serena could only shrug. "I think I did the best I could today," Serena said. She then made the finals of the French Open only to lose another tough match against Garbiñe Muguruza. Serena's coach said the pressure to win twenty-two was everywhere, and if Serena wasn't feeling it, "she would not be human." Serena just praised her opponent and vowed to keep going. "Garbiñe played unbelievable," Serena said. "The only thing I can do is just keep trying."

One thing Serena made sure to do was act with grace and sportsmanship in defeat. While losing, especially in the finals, can be frustrating, it is important not to take anything away from an opponent's accomplishment. It can be hard to turn off that competitive drive, especially in heated matches, but this was something that Richard taught the girls at a young age.

"[It's important to be] genuinely happy at that moment for the people that I lost to," Serena said. "I just felt like, if anything, these ladies inspire me to want to do better. Why would I be jealous of them? I have so many titles, so many Grand Slams, so many things that I'm proud of. I just feel honored that I'm welcoming them to this unique position with open arms."

There was another major development in Serena's life that made winning a Grand Slam or two even more pressing.

In May 2015, Serena was in Rome for the Italian Open. One morning she and a group of friends went to breakfast at a hotel restaurant. They were waiting for more friends to arrive and tried to hold open a table next to them. Then a tall American came in and sat down. His name was Alexis Ohanian, and he was one of the founders of the popular and successful website Reddit. Serena had never heard of Alexis or Reddit. At that moment, she just wanted him to move so the table would be free when her friends arrived. After all, he was alone. He didn't need a big table. One of Serena's friends tried to get him to leave by claiming there was a rat under his table.

"I'm from Brooklyn," Alexis said, according to *Vanity Fair*. "I see rats all the time."

"Oh," Serena said, "you're not afraid of rats?"

When it became clear that Alexis wasn't

moving, Serena decided to have him join their group for breakfast. Alexis was a fan of the NFL and the NBA but had never watched a tennis match before. He did know who Serena Williams was, though, because he'd seen her in commercials, newspapers, and magazines. Meanwhile, Serena knew nothing of Alexis and very little about the technology world that he was famous in. He said he was in Rome for a conference. Serena asked whose speech he'd be attending. Alexis said he was actually the speaker. She quickly realized that he was a big deal.

Serena invited Alexis to watch her match that night, his first tennis match ever. She won, and he was impressed. Alexis and Serena soon began dating and in December 2016, Alexis asked Serena to marry him at the same hotel in Rome where they'd met (he even brought along a plastic rat as a joke).

The couple knew they wanted to start a family, and as Serena entered her midthirties, she decided she didn't want to put that off for much longer. That would mean taking time off for the pregnancy and caring for the newborn. A return to tennis would require a significant comeback both physically and mentally.

While the outside world worried that Serena might not win two more majors before age began to affect her game, Serena suspected that a big change was coming that would take her from the game for a spell and potentially alter her priorities. That made each Grand Slam even more important because there were only so many left.

One of those was 2016 Wimbledon. Serena entered the top seed and then played like it. She roared to the finals, dropping just one set and constantly overwhelming her opponents. In the semifinals, it took her just forty-eight minutes to defeat Elena Vesnina 6–2, 6–0. She won points on 96 percent of her serves. Venus lost in the semifinals, denying another Williams-Williams final (but they would win the doubles title). Instead, Angelique Kerber, who had defeated Serena back in Australia, was waiting. Could she stop the quest for a twenty-second Grand Slam again?

Not this time. Serena continued her great play, and when she hammered home a volley that Kerber couldn't return to win the match, Serena tossed her racket aside and fell to the ground. For a few moments, she just lay on the plush Wimbledon grass as cheers rained down on her. As much as equaling Steffi Graf was satisfying, it was also, after coming so close so many times, a bit of a relief.

"It's been incredibly difficult not to think about

it," Serena said. "I had a couple tries this year. But it makes the victory even sweeter to know how hard I worked for it . . . I have definitely had some sleepless nights."

The US Open was next, but Serena's play and practice were limited due to injuries. She managed to overcome them to reach the semifinals but fell short there. The dream of a twenty-third Grand Slam would have to wait.

Next up was the Australian Open, which takes place in January, so it's winter in the United States but summer down under. The temperatures in Melbourne can soar to more than one hundred degrees, and it feels even hotter when the sun blasts down on the asphalt courts. Serena was always thinking about how to conserve energy.

It became an even bigger priority in 2017 because just days before the start of the tournament, Serena discovered that she was pregnant. She and Alexis, who rushed to Australia to be with her, were overjoyed. They were about to start the family they'd dreamed about.

Since Serena was just a few weeks pregnant, there was still the matter of the Australian Open and the pursuit of that twenty-third Grand Slam. Could she still play? Would it be safe for the baby, let alone her? Mothers-to-be can remain very active during pregnancies, but competing in a Grand Slam in brutal heat is another level. Serena and Alexis kept the pregnancy a secret but had a few doctors check Serena out. They thought it would be grueling, but she would be fine. Serena, knowing a long layoff was coming, decided to go for it.

If she was going to get that twenty-third Grand Slam, it was now or, perhaps, never. No one knew what would happen after she gave birth. To win, however, she needed to forget she was pregnant every time she took the court. If she just played her game, she believed she could win. If she was thinking about the baby, she might alter her style and lose.

Serena was as good as ever. No one could have seen that she was physically pregnant or mentally distracted. She reached the finals without dropping a single set. And there waiting for her, of all people, was Venus. It would be their twenty-eighth head-to-head matchup and the first in a Grand Slam final since 2009 Wimbledon. Venus was thirty-six. Serena was thirty-five. All these years later, the kids from Compton were still controlling the tennis world, just as Richard, who would watch courtside, had predicted.

"I just feel like my dad really had some innovative

things that we worked on and that we always played," Serena said. "He taught us different techniques that no one else was doing. People were like, 'What are you doing? That's not the right way.' But my dad just knew, watched footwork, knew different things that would work better for tennis . . . We definitely were able to revolutionize a lot of things in the game."

Venus had seven Grand Slam titles, ranking her eighth all-time in the Open Era. She had lost, however, to Serena six times in a Slam final, meaning if not for her younger sister, she might have thirteen. Chances to win Grand Slams were rare for Venus at this point. She hadn't been to a final since losing to Serena in 2009 at Wimbledon.

Serena was just as determined as Venus to win. Both sisters were going to bring everything they had. The fans were treated to an incredible match, with long rallies and gut-wrenching shots. Each point felt like the championship hung in the balance. Nothing was conceded. Everything was fought over. Serena often tried to fire herself up with her signature shout, "Come on!"

"Unbearable tension," the announcer on ESPN described it.

Serena won the first set 6–4 and then led 5–4 in

the second. When Venus hit a shot into the net to set up championship point for her younger sister, Serena pumped her first and shouted to herself. "Fight! You fight!" On the next point, Serena hammered a forehand that Venus couldn't fully handle. When the point and championship were won, Serena collapsed on the court. It was part joy, part shock, part exhaustion, both physical and emotional. Rather than share a polite post-match handshake, Venus walked around the net and tightly hugged her sister. Serena could hardly celebrate. She flashed a "2" and a "3" with her fingers to signal her twenty-third Grand Slam victory.

At the trophy presentation, Venus and Serena spent more time talking about each other than themselves. Serena may have won the title, but on this night, the Williams sisters were both champions.

"Serena Williams," Venus said as the crowd cheered. "That's my little sister, guys . . . Serena . . . your win has always been my win. I'm enormously proud of you. You mean the world to me."

"There is no way I would be at twenty-three without her," Serena said of Venus. "There's no way I would be at one without her. There's no way I would have anything without her. She is the only reason I am standing here today. She is the only reason the Williams sisters exist. So thank you, Venus, for inspiring me to be the best player I can be."

The tennis world cheered for Serena's accomplishment. They didn't truly know how impressive it was until later. Serena skipped a couple of WTA events, citing a knee injury, but that wasn't why she was inactive. On April 19, Serena sent out a picture on her Snapchat showing she was pregnant with the caption "20 weeks." She soon deleted it and said sending it was a mistake, but by then it was all over social media.

Fans began calculating the days and quickly realized that back in January, Serena Williams had won a Grand Slam while . . . pregnant. It also meant she was going on maternity leave and wouldn't be competing anytime soon.

On September 1, 2017, Serena gave birth to her daughter, Alexis Olympia Ohanian Jr. Serena called her Olympia. "That was an amazing feeling," Serena told *Vogue*. "And then everything went bad."

"Bad" included the recurrence of blood clots in her lungs just a day after the birth, requiring multiple emergency surgeries. Serena could have died. Her family rushed to the hospital to be around her. She wasn't healthy enough to leave for a week. "Because of all the blood issues," Serena said, "I was really touch and go for a minute." Getting home was only a little better. She was weak from the surgery and the clots and overwhelmed at being a new mother. She could barely walk around the house.

Serena was determined to be a great mother to Olympia but also to return to tennis. She wanted to prove that she could do it. She still had that drive to win. And she wanted to play in front of her daughter. Throughout the fall and winter, she made slow steps to her return. This was the most challenging comeback yet. There were times she was frustrated. There were times she didn't think she could make it. There were times she considered quitting.

She never gave up.

In March, she returned to the WTA, playing in Indian Wells, where fans again cheered her, this time for an entirely new accomplishment. Serena won in straight sets. Then she won her second-round match before losing to Venus in the third. It wasn't the level of tennis Serena wanted to be playing, but the fact that she was playing at all meant the world to her.

"I have a little ways to go," Serena said. "But I'll get there. I'm just going to go for it."

A little less than four months later, Serena was,

indeed, going for it. She had entered Wimbledon and, before the tournament even started, walked out onto Centre Court with Olympia. Serena wanted to show her daughter the place where so many magical moments had happened—Grand Slams and Olympic gold. She wanted to tell her how it had all seemed so far away when she was just a kid from Compton.

"I got a little emotional when I was telling her a story about a girl who had a big dream," Serena said. "I started getting choked up."

Then over the next two weeks, Serena played like the Serena of old. Maybe she wasn't quite as fast or quite as powerful, but she was good enough to keep advancing all the way to the finals. She found herself back on Centre Court in early July, this time playing for another Grand Slam. She would lose to Angelique Kerber in straight sets, but the accomplishment of reaching the final at thirty-six, less than a year after giving birth, inspired the world.

Two months later, Serena made a similar run in the US Open, including beating Venus in the third round. Her return to New York and her favorite tournament drew in huge crowds and high television ratings. She wound up losing in the finals to

Naomi Osaka of Japan, a twenty-year-old who grew up idolizing Serena. The match was marred by an argument between Serena and the umpire, which resulted in Serena being penalized a game. Serena felt the penalty was unfair because male players often argue with even greater intensity with the umpire and aren't penalized. She felt she was being treated differently because she was a woman. No matter the ruling, Osaka was the better player on that night.

The pro-Serena crowd in New York was upset at the controversy, and after the match ended, they began to boo. Serena didn't like that and made sure to silence them. "No more booing . . . This is her first Grand Slam," Serena said. She knew plenty about fans booing, after all. "Congratulations, Naomi!" Serena said.

The crowd responded with cheers. While the argument set off days of debate about who was correct, there was little surprise that Serena would raise such a difficult question or be in the middle of a controversy for speaking her mind and showing her passion. She'd been that way since she was a little girl, sneaking into youth tournaments, battling against her older sister, or fighting for things such as equal prize money for female players.

Her appearances in the Wimbledon and US Open finals so soon after childbirth and the emergency surgeries also cemented Serena's status as a legend, not just in tennis, but in all sports, and not just among women, but among all people. She had recently been asked by a reporter about what she thinks when she hears someone call her "one of the greatest female athletes of all time."

Serena, ever the fiery competitor, ever seeking to establish equality, ever willing to stand up for herself and other minorities, answered simply.

"I prefer the word 'one of the greatest athletes of all time.'"

Instant Replay

1999 US Open Finals:
Serena Williams vs. Martina Hingis

SERENA'S ROAD TO A MAJOR CHAMPIONSHIP BEGAN WHEN SHE WAS A KID.

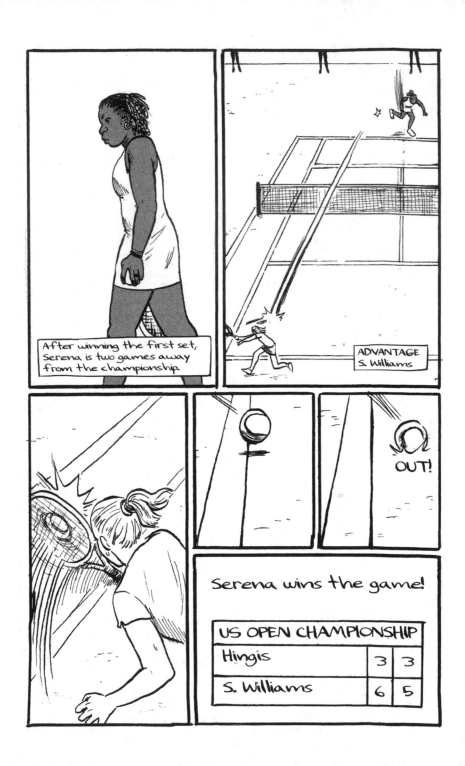

US OPEN	CHAMPIONSHIP
Hingis	4
S. Williams	4

SERENA TAKES
THE LEAD IN
THE TIEBREAKER!

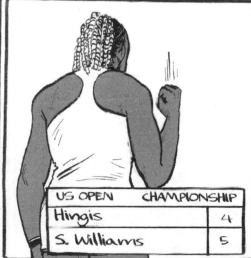

US OPEN	CHAMPIONSHIP
Hingis	4
S. Williams	5

OUT!

Serena wins!

US OPEN	CHAMPIONSHIP		
Hingis		3	6
S. Williams		6	7
	ARTHUR ASHE STADIUM		

The Nonstop Sports Action Continues!

Here's an excerpt of

EPIC ATHLETES
SIMONE BILES

Illustrations by Marcelo Baez

THE 2016 OLYMPICS WOMEN'S GYMNASTICS ALL-AROUND FINAL

1

Golden

SIMONE BILES, IN HER custom-fit, red, white, and blue leotard, stood on one end of the mat, her left hand high in the air, her right resting on her hip.

Twelve thousand fans stared down at her inside Rio Olympic Arena in Brazil, everyone hushed and quiet as they waited for the music to start and Simone to begin a ninety-second floor routine that might tumble her right into history.

The then-nineteen-year-old from the suburbs of Houston, Texas, was in the lead at the women's all-around gymnastics competition at the 2016

Olympics. All that remained was her strongest event—floor. Do it well and she'd be crowned champion.

There were Olympic rings hanging on a banner overhead. There was a gold medal waiting to be hung around someone's neck. There was anticipation in the air as spectators wondered what type of show the greatest gymnast of all time would stage. She was a tiny figure in the middle of a huge arena, an American dynamo who stood just four foot eight.

"I tell people four foot nine sometimes," she once said with a laugh.

To say this was Simone Biles's lifelong dream, the one that powered her through the days at practice when she lacked motivation, wasn't even true. She had never actually dreamed this far. Olympic champion? Gold medalist? The greatest of all time? That was too much to conceive, even on those quiet nights growing up when she tried to fantasize her way to sleep.

No, as a young gymnast, leaping and cartwheeling through recreation classes and local Junior Olympic meets and even as she climbed the competitive national and international ranks, pushing herself more and more, she aspired only to reach the Olympics.

Just getting here was enough. Winning gold? It somehow never crossed her mind.

Simone was a planner. She liked to write down goals in a small notebook she kept in her bedroom back in Spring, Texas. It could be about achieving a certain grade in a certain class, something related to gymnastics, or another milestone. It was a way to keep her focused. It was a way to keep her going.

Yet once she qualified for her first Olympics a few weeks prior to the 2016 games in Rio de Janeiro, there was nothing else she had written down that remained to be accomplished. She had already been national champion four times and world champion three. She had already turned professional. She had already signed contracts that would make her millions in endorsement deals.

Her mother, Nellie, was concerned that Simone might not perform well if she didn't jot down the ultimate goal—Olympic champion in the all-around. That gold signifies the best in the world because it requires each gymnast to perform in all four events—vault, balance beam, uneven bars, and this one, floor exercise. So Nellie encouraged her daughter to put it on paper, make it official.

Simone was hesitant. It seemed unnecessary and

even made her nervous and anxious. She had come to embrace the philosophy of Martha Karolyi, the US national team coordinator and a legendary coach in the sport.

"Martha would say, 'You want to perform like you train. Did you perform like you trained? If you perform like you train, then the judging will work itself out,'" Simone said.

It's a simple lesson that can deliver incredible accomplishments. Do what you can do and don't stress about anything else.

"If I do my job, I do my job," Simone said. "There is nothing I can do to control the scores."

So Simone would only meet her mother halfway. She did write down a new goal, but it had nothing to do with medals or scores or sticking the landing on an Amanar.

"I will make you proud," Simone wrote to her mother.

That was it. That was all. Nellie could only smile when she read it. Simone could have fallen fifty times on her floor routine and she would still be proud of her daughter.

Ron and Nellie Biles were not Simone's birth parents. They were, originally, her grandparents.

Ron Biles had a daughter from a previous relationship named Shanon, who had given birth to four children, including Simone, the third child. Shanon and the kids lived in Ohio, but when Shanon struggled with alcohol and drug addiction, eventually child services said she was an unfit mother and took her children from her, putting them temporarily in foster care.

Ron and Nellie had married after his first relationship broke off, and they were living in Texas at the time. When Shanon was unable to care for her kids, the pair stepped in and adopted the two youngest, Simone and her little sister, Adria. The two older children went with another relative. It wasn't planned this way, but Grandma and Grandpa officially and legally became Simone's mom and dad. Ron and Nellie already had two older boys and now the family was unexpectedly bigger, and given Simone's natural interest in flips and twists, bouncier.

Neither Ron nor Nellie knew anything about gymnastics when Simone and Adria first began going to a local gym to burn off excess energy. They certainly never expected to be here, at the Olympics, staring down at their daughter who was on the verge of winning the all-around gold. It wasn't the athletic success that made them love her, though. It was everything else.

"We have so much satisfaction from all our kids," Ron Biles said. "We love family and everything involved with it. We share all the special moments together and this is a pretty special one."

Down on that mat, Simone was trying to remain calm. She had trained since she was six years old to get to this spot. She had always been a pint-size powerhouse, always small for her age. Yet in elementary school, she was often stronger than the boys and had no problem showing them.

She was pure muscle, with ripped arms and springy legs that launched her into the air. She had a core so strong she could twist in midair almost at will. She also possessed an unteachable ability to sense where she was while in flight.

The routine she was about to attempt was one of the most technically challenging runs of skills in the history of the sport. The Olympics were home to the best gymnasts on earth, yet no other gymnast present would even attempt such a difficult feat.

Simone wasn't just going to try it. She was going to try to do it perfectly.

It began with a full-twisting double layout, where

a gymnast flips in the air with her legs completely straightened out (rather than bending her knees). Next up, a double laid-out salto (a flip with the legs tucked to the chest) with a half twist, a move so hard that no one had ever landed it in a World Championship until Simone had done so in 2013. As a result, it was known as "the Biles."

The Biles led Simone into a split jump and later there was a tumbling pass with a double-double (two somersaults with two full twists) and then the finale with a tucked full-in (two somersaults and a twist with legs pressed together and to the chest). In between the four tumbling runs, there were other required moves, choreographed dancing with a salsa flair, and a beaming smile to engage the crowd.

The routine was so demanding that it earned a 6.800 degree of difficulty, which is one part of a gymnastics score. The other is how the judges think you executed it. No one else in the meet had a difficulty score higher than 6.600.

Simone hadn't lost an individual all-around competition since 2013, yet this one, the Olympic all-around, hadn't been easy. She had led after the first event, vault, but then fell behind Russia's Aliya Mustafina after the second rotation, bars, when

Aliya put up an impressive 15.666, a full 0.7 higher than Simone.

The crowd in Rio de Janeiro mumbled in surprise when Aliya took the overall lead, 30.866 to 30.832. Everyone had expected Simone to run away with the gold, just like always. Now they were wondering if a historic upset was in the making.

Simone's personal coach, Aimee Boorman, told her to just stick with her training. Teammate Aly Raisman, who was also competing in the all-around, high-fived her and tried to pump her up.

And Bela and Martha Karolyi, the legendary husband-and-wife coaching duo who essentially ran USA Gymnastics, reminded Simone that since bars were her weakest event and Aliya's strongest, there was no need to panic. There was plenty of time during the final two events—beam and floor—to retake the lead.

"That made this competition so spicy, so beautiful," said Bela Karolyi, who for over forty years had coached many of the greatest gymnasts of all time. "The beam is the leaning point [though]. The left or the right. The best-trained gymnast stays on the beam."

Well, beam was next. And before Simone's routine,

she heard Nellie Biles shout a saying that she'd been screaming to Simone her entire competitive career.

"You've got this, Simone!" Nellie said.

That was more than enough for Simone. As with the floor event to come, she benefited from having a far more difficult technical routine in the beam than her competitors, tougher than anyone else was even willing to attempt.

She then drilled it, proving herself, as Bela said, "the best-trained gymnast," and scoring a 15.433 to Aliya's 13.866.

Once again Simone was in the lead, this time by a commanding 1.533 points (while that may seem like a small margin, it's a *huge* lead in gymnastics).

By the time she stood on the mat to start her floor routine as the last performer of the night, she knew gold was there for the taking. Aliya's overall score had even been passed by Aly Raisman, thanks to Aly's tremendous execution on a very difficult floor routine.

Aly Raisman was competing in her second Olympics after winning a gold medal in 2012. She was famous and a hero to gymnasts around the world. Yet she knew that she wasn't going to beat Simone's score. Simone's lead was so large, and her routine so challenging, she could fall multiple times and still win.

Aly was fine with that. She, along with everyone else in attendance, knew there really was no competing with Simone Biles.

"[US teammate] Laurie Hernandez said to me, 'If you get silver, you're the best because Simone doesn't count,'" Aly said with a laugh. "Her start value is [so much] higher than me so I know I can't beat her."

Simone didn't like that kind of talk—she wanted to encourage her teammates. She loved them and was proud of how good they were. "I get more excited when they win," she said. When Aly finished her brilliant floor routine to assure her at least a silver medal, she cried in delight, with Simone hugging and celebrating with her.

Suddenly Simone was fighting back tears of joy for Aly. "I thought, 'Oh my God, she's going to make me cry before my floor,'" Simone later said with a laugh. "And that wasn't going to be good."

With what felt like the whole world watching Simone, it was not the time to think of Aly or anyone else. This was about doing what she had trained to do. This was the time to concentrate. This was the time to win.

As the music started, the anxiety melted away and a huge smile broke out on her face.

"That is all we needed to see," her older brother, Adam, who was also there cheering her on, said. "As long as she has a smile on her face, we know she is in a good place."

Soon she was sprinting down the mat for her first tumbling run and springing into her round-off. Her muscles were trained. Her mind was clear.

"Sometimes nothing goes through my mind," Simone said. "When I tumble, I just tumble."

She soared nearly ten feet into the air before landing cleanly, with just a small hop to take away the momentum. The crowd roared. Soon she was repeating it . . . the buildup of speed, the concentration, the flying toward glory before ending with a sound, sharp landing.

Just like that, Simone Biles knew she was going to win gold.

"Once the first two passes were out of the way, I knew I was good," she said.

Everyone knew. The crowd was now on its collective feet, waving flags and roaring in delight. This was the ultimate performance, a dream combination of skill and entertainment. Simone leaping. Simone flipping. Simone in total command.

"The joy," Bela Karolyi said of watching it. "The satisfaction."

"Pride," her dad said.

This is what Simone wanted—to perform for the beauty of performing. Not for judges. Not for medals. She had always loved gymnastics for the sake of gymnastics. She hadn't reached the national team until she was fifteen, late for the great ones. No one had ever doubted her ability, but coaches were frustrated that she sometimes wanted gymnastics to be more about fun than just work.

Simone liked to smile at practice. She liked to laugh. "Gymnastics is supposed to be fun," she'd say.

Eventually her performances got so good and her technical ability so precise that even Martha Karolyi gave up trying to rein her in. Martha was a taskmaster. She was forever pushing gymnasts to be better and better. She wasn't much for laughs and smiles during training.

Simone, though . . . well, Simone could pretty much do whatever she wanted. The performance, and the results, spoke for her.

"Simone Biles is the biggest talent," Martha said. "Combined with the very good discipline of work and great preparation for consistency, she is the best."

By the time her routine ended, Simone was beaming. She rushed off the mat and hugged Coach Aimee, hugged Martha, and eventually wound up in a prolonged hug with Aly. Four years prior, she'd watched Aly win team gold for the Americans at the 2012 London Olympics. Simone considered Aly a role model.

At the time, there was no guarantee that Simone would ever make the senior national team, or World Championships, or these Olympics. She was fifteen and still hadn't broken through. Now four years later, there they were, the two of them awaiting the final scores.

When the scores were presented, the pair hugged even tighter. Simone had scored a 15.933 on floor, the highest score by any competitor in any event that night. That meant she won all-around gold over Aly by a whopping 2.100 margin.

The 2.1 differential wasn't just the largest margin of victory in the history of the Olympic women's all-around. It was larger than the combined margins of victory of every Olympic all-around, 1980–2012. By comparison, Gabby Douglas won all-around gold in 2012 by just 0.259.

Simone had blown out the competition. She would climb atop the podium and receive her medal, and yet even with all that she'd accomplished, she said she didn't feel a whole lot different.

"I'm still the same old Simone," she said.

The road to gold hadn't been easy. It had been full of twists and turns, laden with doubts and down periods.

She had made it, though. She had fulfilled her goal of reaching the Olympics.

There was also that goal she'd written down in her notebook.

"I will make you proud," she had promised her mother.

Up in the stands, with her parents and siblings crying tears of happiness, there was no doubt she had done that, too.

Hungry for More EPIC ATHLETES?
Look Out for These Superstar
Biographies, in Stores Now!

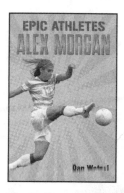

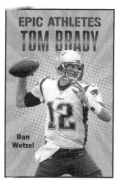

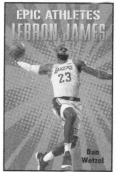

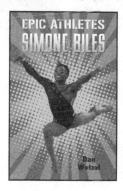